RESCUE, RESTORE, REDECORATE

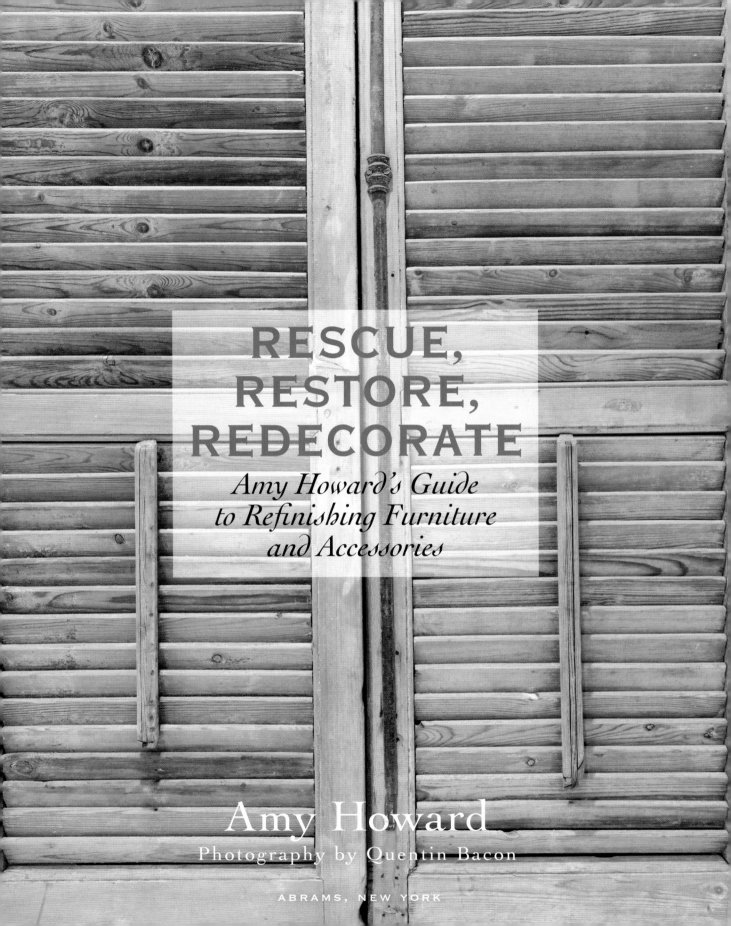

RESCUE, RESTORE, REDECORATE

*Amy Howard's Guide
to Refinishing Furniture
and Accessories*

Amy Howard

Photography by Quentin Bacon

ABRAMS, NEW YORK

To the love of my life, Gene. From unloading trucks, carrying heavy books from the Paris flea market, setting up displays at midnight, traipsing through flea markets and antique malls all over the globe, hauling furniture and redoing it more times than we could count, to rescuing and building thirteen homes in twenty-six years—and having a smile on your face the entire time. Without you, truly none of this would have ever happened. Your unconditional love gives me the feeling that I can do anything.

TABLE OF CONTENTS

INTRODUCTION

Imagine your favorite place in the whole world. In my case, I would be sitting in a quaint French café, sipping espresso and enjoying a decadent meal with my husband. If I close my eyes, I can almost take in the aroma of freshly baked bread, or hear the sounds of laughter filling that bustling spot. I can almost see the zinc-topped bar, and feel the painted chairs, worn with age and smooth under my hands. And there's a warm glow over everything—that Parisian light melting through the window—that makes us feel like part of a long, wonderful story, yet entirely alive in this moment.

When we surround ourselves at home with things we love—things that have a history—it makes each day not only more comfortable, but also more beautiful and meaningful. There's no reason you can't have a chair with a patina of age like the one at your favorite restaurant, or a dresser that's as gorgeous as the one you've been coveting in the window of that antiques store. Not only can you have pieces like these—you can make them look that way yourself. That's what this book will teach you.

Now, of course, being able to renovate furniture that appears to belong in the finest store or the most luxurious home means you will earn some serious bragging rights (especially when you bought the original piece for a song!). The pride that comes from your guests' awed responses can be very satisfying. But even more, there's the satisfaction that comes from knowing you made something special with your own two hands, something that you can use and enjoy every day.

Your home represents you and everything you hope to convey, and even having a single piece in it that you've restored is an expression of your personality and what makes you happy. If you've never rescued a flea market find or an heirloom in need of attention, it may feel like a challenge to know where to begin. Here's the good news: You can start small, quick, and cheap. It's likely that the design styles you love most are right under your nose. Maybe they are pieces passed down to you that you'd cherish if only they had a little refresh. Maybe they're waiting around the corner at an antiques market you can pop into this weekend, or at a yard sale you'll drive by. The world is full of promising items that have been discarded. You just have to look a little further than your coffee table catalog; and that's what this book will teach you to do as well. It doesn't have to cost you a lot (though I promise it will look as if it did). It doesn't have to take you a lot of time (you'll be amazed at how little time it takes to renovate pieces you'll want to keep forever).

Over the years, I have found that learning to rescue, restore, and redecorate furniture and objects begins with tapping into your imagination. Through the projects in this book, I will teach you how to recognize potential beyond what your eyes behold. Instead of seeing a wood chair in a boring shade of brown . . . or an unremarkable mirrored tabletop . . . or a dated dresser with dull hardware . . . you will begin to see each item as a canvas for your creativity. You'll start to think, "I would adore this chair in a soft Swedish blue," or "This tabletop could look like the mercury glass walls in my favorite bistro," or "That dresser is crying out for some swanky fire-engine-red lacquer and gilded handles." Once you get some practice, you'll realize that any of these transformations can happen over a weekend, for less than the cost of one dinner out.

Not only that, but every piece will have a story. This is true even if you are working with new materials, not antiques. No matter how the piece became yours, you will have rescued it from being ordinary, cookie-cutter, or dated. You will have restored and redecorated it to be extraordinary.

In this book, I will introduce you to seventeen different categories of finishes, from gilding to painting to antiquing a mirror. The eighteen step-by-step projects often mix and match several techniques. Each project will build your skills, and by the time you've made your way through the pages that follow, you will have mastered a repertoire of finishes. To me, this is where the most fun comes in: Once you have that arsenal of techniques, you can dream up—and make—your own custom creations. I hope you'll experiment, combining several techniques on one item or trying an unexpected finish on an old piece to give it new life. I hope you'll walk away with a new sense of confidence, and a new level of connoisseurship about what makes a home beautiful. Most of all, I hope you'll see that learning these amazing, easy, versatile finishes is just the start.

THE RESCUE RESTORE REDECORATE LIFESTYLE

When I have guests over, they always notice my treasures. Sometimes, their eyes go to the creamy-white table with gold accents in my entryway. Other times, they can't help touching the antique mirrored tray under the glasses of sweet tea, or the deliciously shiny blue lacquered nightstand. They often ask me where I find all of my amazing goodies. For years, I would just smile and say, "Oh, here and there really." I had traveled around my city—and a few others—curating a little list of the best shops with the best finds. But one day, something changed in my outlook. Maybe it was that I had ended up gathering so many treasures that I had to start selling some. Maybe it was that my heart ached to think of all of the incredible pieces of furniture being wasted, when they could have been transformed by a little TLC. But I think that most of all, it was when I realized how much joy it gave me to transform them myself. I started teaching my friends, and then many other people, how to rescue furniture, restore it with antique-style finishes, and redecorate with it. An all-new level of joy came through teaching others to create their own treasures. These joys are at the heart of the Rescue Restore Redecorate lifestyle. It's not just about a single craft project, it's also about crafting a beautiful life with your own hands. It's about tapping into the potential of what you see. Saving money and reducing waste is one part of it (and one that means a lot to me personally). And, of course, who doesn't love a good Cinderella story? There are so many pieces out there that just need a bit of love to become as breathtaking as a belle at the ball.

My home is full of stories and memories. I have raised my babies there, held countless family dinners, and embraced the people I love time and time again. I'm sure your home already has many stories to tell. Can you ever have too many stories? Too many things that mean the world to you? When you rescue, restore, and redecorate a vintage piece, you not only bring a new chair or table or dresser or mirror into your home. You bring in a new story, as well. You're giving something old a new life, one that makes your own life even richer and better. That's the *Rescue, Restore, Redecorate* lifestyle. Welcome home.

You can have a chair with a patina like the one at your favorite restaurant, or a dresser like the one at the antiques store. You can you have pieces like these—and make them look that way yourself. This book will teach you how.

CHAPTER 1
THE THRILL OF THE HUNT

When people ask me my favorite pastime, I say, "There's no play I've been to, no musical, and no movie that's as exciting as the thrill of the hunt."

My husband, Gene, and I were planning a trip to New York. "We could take that late flight out of Memphis on Sunday evening," he suggested. But we looked at each other, thinking the same thing: "Let's leave on Saturday morning instead and catch all the street markets in New York!"

Any city we go to, anywhere we travel, we always think about the outdoor flea markets and vendors. We love forging that emotional connection to the city. And most of all, we love not knowing what we'll encounter! That thrill of possibility . . .

The same thing also happens whenever we go to an estate sale or even when we find a treasure on the side of the road and maneuver it into our car. In all of these situations, you have to act fast because you never know what might happen if you wait; 10 minutes later, the object of your interest will be gone. This heightens the excitement, of course.

I also love the pride that comes with our finds (and what a steal they were!). Isn't it funny that when we buy new furniture, we never walk around saying, "I paid ___ dollars for that chair!," but when you rescue and restore furniture, it's a badge of honor to say, "I got this for ten dollars!" or "I found this on the side of the road!"?

For me, the greatest thrill of the hunt is learning to see each piece for its potential and taking a chance on it (because, if you are like me, you believe you can turn it into something amazing). You no longer see the state it is in; you envision it 100 percent restored, and just how it will look in your own home. The utilitarian aspect becomes less important. Of course you'll judge it on size and scale and how you could use it, but now what you're really dreaming about is the detailing: how you could paint it, lacquer it, gild it, or deck it out with stripes. The more you get into the hunt, and restoring furniture, the more you'll develop a connoisseurship and a discerning eye. When you look at furniture, you'll be able to recognize character, when a piece has good bones and could be beautiful with the right care. Here are some tips to help you in your hunt.

CARPE DIEM

The best time to buy an antique or one-of-a-kind piece is right when you see it and know that you love it. After all, there may not be another chance. At street markets or flea markets, the dealers are usually set up by 6 A.M., and there will be people walking right behind you, ready to buy. You've got to develop the instinct to make quick decisions! When Gene and I are shopping, we sometimes split up to cover more ground, and use walkie-talkies. If I see something I like, I'll message Gene or take a picture. Sometimes I don't even have that much time, and it's a now-or-never proposition, so I go with my gut. If it's early in the morning, or a big field sale like Brimfield, I may have to pay full price, but most of the time, I ask the dealer what his price is, and I haggle. If he's got it at $45, I ask him, "Would you consider $35?" Knowing I got a great deal can be part of the fun.

FLEA MARKET TIP *Carry cash with you, and don't be afraid to let them see your twenties, to create a sense of urgency. If you find two or three things you like from one dealer and group them together, they'll usually be open to giving you a better deal.*

If the dealer is willing, I will often take a picture of him or her and ask to hear the story of where they found the pieces I have chosen and what they know about them. It's also a great way to develop relationships that can be important as you continue to collect. You will find yourself drawn to certain dealers' aesthetics. Get their information so that you can contact them in the future. Anytime I go to Atlanta or New York, I contact my dealers and ask if I can come by their warehouse. When I go to estate sales and there are forty to fifty people in there, I've got to make decisions quickly. But now that I've nurtured relationships with people who run estate sales, they call me because they know what I like, and they'll ask, "Do you want to come the day before?" I know I'll have to pay full price, but that's part of the privilege of getting the first shot at some special items.

If you like a more leisurely pace, an antiques mall is another good option. On Saturday mornings, I love going to the one on Summer Avenue in Memphis. It's a time to wear tennis shoes and a baseball cap, since I'll be digging and haggling. A lot of the dealers know me and that I need a good price, and I can browse without feeling rushed.

The time to buy is when you see it and love it.

PASSION TO PROFESSION

No child says, "I want to be an antiques dealer when I grow up." My sister was a nurse anesthetist and her husband was an architect, but they learned that they loved going to London and buying antiques for their home. They loved it so much that they wanted to buy more than they needed! That's how their passion became a profession.

If you discover you have that kind of passion for the hunt, for discovering the treasures-in-waiting and making them beautiful, people might see your home and say, "I could never do that." And you may find yourself replying, "I can make you a piece just like it! I'll paint it for you!" It will be so natural. Suddenly you may have a garage full of furniture you can sell! That's what happened to every antiques dealer I've ever talked to. They loved collecting treasures, and when they had nowhere to put them, it became a business.

ANTIQUES MALL TIP *Nine times out of ten, antiques malls will offer 10 to 20 percent off to designers and dealers. You'll just need a tax ID to qualify, and then you can ask about a "trade discount."*

A lady at one of the workshops I teach told me that she had worked hard for thirty years and was very tired. "But I've started going to these auctions of furniture . . ." she added—and her eyes lit up. "I've never had a passion like that before." And I said, "Why not see where it takes you?"

If you're reading this book, you may be perfectly content if it teaches you to rescue a piece or two and turn them into something that gives you a thrill. Don't be surprised, though, if the result gives others a thrill, too. You may start fielding requests to accompany your friends on their treasure hunts, or they may ask you to make them a piece just like yours. This could be your opportunity to step out and start something new that could bloom into a new career. Whether you do it for fun or turn it into a new vocation, I think you'll find a lot of joy in sharing your passion. I know I do.

CHAPTER 2
THE CREATIVE PANTRY

In my kitchen pantry at home, I always have onions, garlic, spices, and grains at the ready—staples that mean I can make almost anything I want by adding fresh vegetables or meat. My pantry space is fun to look at, too—I like seeing my salts and seasonings and herbs! From the moment I began to write this book, I thought of it like a cookbook. I loved the idea of sharing my recipes for furniture finishes with you, with the ingredients and instructions you need to create a delicious result—as well as the story behind that particular project, such as why I chose the pieces and finishes you see. And I don't know about you, but now that I'm comfortable in the kitchen, I sometimes like to experiment with my favorite recipes—adding a different spice here, an extra dash of vanilla there. The same is true here: There is plenty of encouragement to substitute the paint color that speaks most to you, to mix and match techniques from one project to the other, to improvise to your heart's content. All of this will seem so easy once you've built your own repertoire of finishes and combinations, which is my dream for this book and for you. So, to begin, let's talk about what you'll need in your creative pantry.

VISUAL INVENTORY

First, you need a place to store everything. I like to be able to take a visual inventory at a glance, so I prefer an industrial metal rack to a cabinet. The openness of the metal rack is useful, as is having it on rollers so that I can move it around my studio space. Additionally, whenever I have a basket of materials for a current project on my work surface or on my shelving, I create a laminated paper label identifying what items the basket contains. That way everything has a dedicated place, and I (and everyone working on projects with me) know where the milk paint goes, where the container of scissors lives, etc. Seeing the whole visual inventory, with everything neat and labeled, not only takes away the stress of searching all over for missing supplies; it also tempts you to get creative.

ROOM OF YOUR OWN *One idea that's become popular in recent years is the "She Shed." If you have a separate space big enough for your supplies and your pieces, you could run with this idea and create a wonderful home for your creativity with shelves, clear boxes, and all of your supplies organized by category and proudly on display so that your brushes, your metallic powders, your pigments can inspire you.*

STOCKED AND STORED TO LAST

Just as with cooking ingredients, there are staples I always like to have in my creative pantry, things like paint thinner and waxes. I also regularly buy unusual supplies for my pantry that I don't have a need for yet because they intrigue me or spark my imagination. I've bought brushes and said, "Maybe I can use these later" (and, somehow, I always do). One time in New Orleans, I bought red and ochre pigments from a woman who had found them in Morocco. They just called to me and I thought, these need to go in my creative pantry. Later, I used them to create a one-of-a-kind Venetian plaster wall. Give yourself permission to buy the essentials as well as some items that will allow you to play and dream in good time, when you're ready to find a use for them.

HERE'S WHAT'S IN MY CREATIVE PANTRY:

- Paints and paint pigments: milk (casein) paint powders, natural chalk-based (calcium carbonate) paints

- Lacquers (in aerosol spray cans)

- Waxes

- Gilding size (see Gilding Like a Pro, page 49)

- Metallic leaf: gold leaf, silver leaf, rose gold leaf, variegated copper leaf (I like having three or four kinds at any time, but if you're just starting out, I recommend starting with gold leaf. Metallic leaf comes in both booklets and loose sheets; I recommend booklets. See Gilding Like a Pro, page 49)

- Mica powders

- Brushes: flat bristle brushes in nylon, synthetic, ox hair, sable; flat foam brushes; round/slender, tapered artist's brushes for striping and detail work; larger brushes for graining

- Tools, such as a screwdriver, hammer, and measuring tape; optional but nice to have: paint-only blender (see following tip), airless paint sprayer

- Paint thinner

- Lacquer thinner

- Gentle liquid soaps

- Gentle degreaser

- Clean, lint-free rags

FOR PAINT ONLY *Although you can make the projects without one, I highly recommend having a dedicated blender for mixing paints and plaster. You don't want to be borrowing things from your kitchen (or putting paint in the blender you use for your morning smoothie!); instead, buy or allocate inexpensive items specifically for your creative pantry. I often pick up a blender at a garage sale for a couple dollars for this purpose; if it breaks, no big loss and there's always another one a few bucks away!*

You will pay more for higher-quality tools, but your supplies will have a big impact on the success of your craft and your finishes. It's also important to treat them with care and make them last. Well-cared-for brushes will be usable for years. Here's how to maintain them:

CLEANING BRUSHES: When you're working with water-based paints, all the care you'll need is gentle soap and water. (I use Dove liquid dishwashing soap.) I hold my brush under running warm tap water, and I run my fingers, with a bit of soap on them, through the bristles, trying to keep them together, not splayed or stippled. You may need to wash the brush three or four times to remove darker paint colors. Then shake most of the water out, and allow the brush to air-dry.

Most waxes are petroleum-based, so you must clean brushes you've used in them with a solvent-based cleaner or thinner (within 30 minutes for light-colored or liming waxes, within 5 minutes if possible for darker waxes). If you're using an oil-based gilding size, it also needs to be washed out of your brushes within 30 minutes (I use a water-based size most often). You may want to keep a cup of water (for water-based paint brushes) or paint thinner (for oil-based paint brushes) handy while working with your finishes, and rest your brush in the cup between uses so that the paint doesn't harden on your brush. Many times, I work with two brushes simultaneously—one resting in the appropriate solution, one active.

STORING BRUSHES: Store them upright so that the bristles get proper air and keep their shape. Especially with fine-artist's brushes, keep the plastic sleeve they came in, and after they have dried, put them back in the sleeve.

I also recommend labeling your brushes for a particular use so that you only put oil-based paint on this one and water-based paint on that one. You'll be using cleaners to remove the residues left from oily products, and crossing between different types of cleaners may harm the brush. In permanent marker, label the handles by their use: "light wax brush," "dark wax brush," "paintbrush," and so on.

THE RIGHT CONTAINER

For some antiquing and refinishing materials, any old can or bowl will do. For others, it's important to use a specific kind of container that won't react with the solvent.

PAINTS (CHALK-BASED OR MILK): You don't have to worry about reactivity with these paints; feel free to use styrofoam or paper bowls, glass containers, plastic cups, metal cans, and the like.

ZINC ANTIQUING SOLUTION: It's important to put this into a plastic or glass container—definitely not metal (no coffee cans!), since the zinc antiquing solution can react with it.

ANTIQUING GLAZE: Paper or styrofoam containers are safe options.

MIRROR STRIPPING SOLUTION: Use glass or metal, not plastic, to avoid reactions.

TIME TO PLAY

I promised you that once you got your creative pantry in order, you would have more time to play and invent. Before I paint a piece, I always go to my creative pantry and take a peek, imagining the finishes individually and in combination. I'll experiment with different layering techniques to come up with something new. I like working with unusual, special items like mica powders and paint pigments because of their depth and history. They've been used for hundreds, maybe thousands, of years, and I love knowing that I'm pulling from the historical elements of finishes and the sophistication of those finishes (sometimes dreaming of Versailles, sometimes of a rustic inn set in the mountains of Tuscany). It's easy to go with premixed or off-the-shelf varieties, but my hope is that through this process, you'll start feeling comfortable enough to step outside of your comfort zone and experiment, to see how exciting it can be!

In the following chapter, you'll learn the need-to-knows and good-to-knows to ensure success with the restoring and refinishing techniques and materials.

An eighteenth-century fragment became part of a console and was given new life with a coat of milk paint and detailed gilding.

CHAPTER 3
A REPERTOIRE OF FINISHES: THE BASICS AND BEYOND

No two objects or pieces of furniture you come across will be identical. Some will be very ornate, carved, and detailed; others will be smoother and more modern. There will be different species of woods, and pieces from different periods, Victorian to midcentury modern to early seventies. As you do more and more hunting, and more and more rescuing, you'll see those things, but you'll also be looking at the bones, the shapes, the sizes, the scale. Your new reaction will be "What could I do to that to make it mine?" Push the limits of how each piece can look different. Take the drawers off the nightstand and put a basket in the bottom of it. Remove the doors and paint the inside. Consider gilding the hardware, or changing it entirely. When would something look good in milk paint? When would it benefit from the gleam of lacquer? It's about your imagination, not just throwing on a coat of paint, or covering an ugly, drab, or stained finish. It might even mean customizing a generic piece you got at a big-box store. The goal is to elevate the piece and make it incredibly special, in your own way.

BEYOND A COAT OF PAINT

In the seventies, everything matched. You would buy a bedroom set and the dresser matched the nightstands, the nightstands matched the bed. Now the elements of good taste lean toward an eclectic, collected mix. A lot of people who have that old, matchy-matchy bedroom set wonder what they should do with it. My answer: finishes, of course. But don't feel that because the set matches, it must all receive the same simple painted finish!

Painting a piece of furniture is satisfying. A lot of people say afterward, "That was great! The before-and-after was really fun, and I loved the transformation." But then comes the tricky part: making something look authentically aged. I may get in trouble for saying this, but I've seen a lot of people use a chalk-based paint on their piece, and then try to create wear and give it some age by sanding it in random places, and it ends up looking like a wild animal was let loose on it and chewed it up!

Now, you know I love that they tried. But just as I'm going to help train your eye to find pieces with great potential, I'm also going to help train your refinishing skills so that what you create looks sophisticated, like it's aged over many decades. You'll see that's how the pedigreed, fine, collector's-quality pieces of furniture look—as if the piece was used, and it has worn naturally. It would wear around the hardware—the handles and escutcheons (the flat metal around the handles), it would wear where the piece was touched, maybe where the cabinet door closed, where an arm rested or a foot tapped against a leg many times. Thinking about

how that piece would have been used will help you decide on the finish.

Sometimes a piece may just need a soft white cerusing wax (also known as a liming wax, which is a cloudy white and highlights the grain of the wood). Sometimes you may want a piece to look antiqued, so you could do a light and dark wax mix. Sometimes you might want to age the wood to add character, or gild the hardware to give it an elegant shimmer. By building a repertoire of finishes and understanding the specific properties of each, you'll learn what they could add to a piece, and how you can make it much more special, much more interesting, than with regular paint alone.

RRR TECHNIQUE BASICS

In my workshops, I often show people how to gild. When I take that gold leaf out and they see the fine tissue flapping in the breeze, they get so nervous. "How am I going to take something that is so fluid and tricky and work with it? How can I be sure I'll end up with something I'll be happy with?" I've watched them struggle, and a lot of the fear is in their heads: "I'm not creative, I can't do this." But as I guide them through the challenges and opportunities, it becomes

I love creating finishes on small samples to decide what will go best on a piece before I restore it. A combination of stain and wax (or wax and paint)—as in many of the examples here—can work wonders in suggesting age. 1. Trompe l'oeil with milk paint, 2. Wood stain and cerusing wax, 3. Cerusing wax, 4. Milk paint, 5. Better with Age, 6. Wood stain, 7. Better with Age on pine, 8. Wood stain and cerusing wax, 9. Milk paint with wax

second nature. Getting over the fear factor of something you've never done before, or been exposed to, helps you to realize, "This is really fun and easy!"

That's why I think that one of the best ways to learn is to dive into a project and see where it takes you (with plenty of guidance along the way, of course). Before you begin, however, here is an overview of the finishes you'll be learning much more about in the following chapters, and some important basics to ensure safe and sound results:

PAINT

Milk paint (also known as casein paint) adds a beautiful depth to a piece when it's layered and antiqued. It's great for giving items that have had everyday use a rich, historical look.

Chalk-based paints (also known as calcium carbonate paints) will be a bit more opaque, less subtle. I love them because of how quickly they can transform an old, tired piece into something stunning.

Typical milk-based or chalk-based finishes are best when you want the piece to have a provincial, antiqued feel, or when the piece already has wonderful details you wish to highlight, but even a very simple, primitive or midcentury chest or table can be beautiful dressed up in paint. As you may have guessed by now, and as you'll see in the projects, I often use paint as a springboard and then add accents like waxes to suggest aging or glittery gold leaf for contrast.

FOR YOUR SAFETY: I recommend choosing natural chalk-based and milk-based paints, which are free of VOCs and harmful fumes.

Because they're safe, you can easily apply either kind of natural paint indoors, but make sure to protect all surrounding surfaces from drips and splatters.

FOR THE BEST RESULTS: Natural chalk-based paint is thick and durable because of the calcium carbonate it contains. It is normal for this heavy sediment to settle at the bottom of the can during storage. Turn your paint can upside down 30 minutes before starting your project to mix things up. Before using, stir it until it's smooth.

When you're using chalk-based paint on fabric such as vinyl (as in the Donovan chairs, page 82), it's best to dilute it in a ratio of 4 parts paint to 1 part warm tap water (for example, for every 16 ounces [480 ml] of paint, you would dilute it with 4 ounces [120 ml] water). (The same ratio applies if you are diluting chalk-based paint to use in an airless sprayer.) The exception to the fabric rule is when you are painting a lampshade and want the paint to be thinner and less opaque so that the light will still shine through the silk blend (or other fabric) of the shade (as in the Augustus lamp, page 78). In this case, dilute the paint in a ratio of 7 parts paint to 3 parts warm tap water (for example, for every 7 ounces [210 ml] of paint, dilute with 3 ounces [90 ml] of water).

Synthetic brushes such as those with nylon bristles will help ensure a smooth application. Apply the paint in long, even strokes, overlapping the edge of each new stroke with the previous one. Once you've applied a full coat of paint, do not brush paint over it again; this is called "double processing" and not only delays the drying time, but also moves hardening paint around, resulting in a bumpy finish.

Milk-based paints come in a powder form that gets mixed with an equal amount of warm tap water. Milk paints don't contain an adherent the way chalk-based paints do. This means that milk paints work beautifully when applied directly to raw wood pieces that they can penetrate, but in projects where we're painting a piece that already has a finish on it, we'll often apply a base coat of chalk-based paint beforehand.

THE GOLDILOCKS PRINCIPLE
Whenever you work with solutions, from paints to glazes, from size to waxes, you'll achieve the best results if you make sure your brush, sponge, or other application tool has just the right amount of material on it. Throughout the projects, I'll remind you to remove the excess (called "offloading") on a handy surface such as the lip of the paint can or the wax container. When that's not an option, a square of clean cardboard often makes a good alternative.

Premixing a milk paint solution of 1 part warm tap water and 1 part milk paint powder the night before a big project allows everything to settle and meld into a buttery smooth consistency. A Mason jar with a lid is a good option for premixing. Add the powder and water and shake well with the lid on. Strain the solution through cheesecloth into a clean container and let it sit overnight. It's best never to paint when air bubbles are present, and it's important to stir the paint every time before you dip the brush into it because the paint will quickly separate into pigment and water.

If you store your milk paint in an airtight container in the refrigerator, it will last for 1 to 2 weeks. For a seamless application, return the solution to room temperature, stir it thoroughly, and strain it through a cheesecloth before use. Lastly, if you find your milk paint has thickened during use, mix a little water back into the solution. Natural-bristle brushes are preferred for use with milk paint, though synthetic brushes work fine.

LACQUER

This high-gloss finish is great for pieces that are not too large, such as lamps, accent tables, maybe a chair with a great silhouette. (You might not want to have an enormous, shiny piece of furniture dominating your room.) Could you use lacquer on a credenza in your dining room? Certainly, but you'll need to take into account the scale of the credenza in conjunction with the mirror or artwork above it; we'll talk about how to make these kinds of decisions in Chapter 11: Crafting a Beautiful Life (page 183).

FOR YOUR SAFETY: It's important to spray the lacquer only in a well-ventilated area, as the fumes can be dangerous.

FOR THE BEST RESULTS: Successful lacquer requires a completely smooth surface, free of dust and other particles, because lacquer shows every imperfection. Before you begin spraying your object or piece with lacquer, it's crucial to clean the surface well. While ventilation is important, you'll want to apply the spray lacquer in a breeze-free area so that no new dirt or other particles stick to the wet lacquer. You'll also sand between coats to get rid of bumps that sneak in.

WAX

Wax is well known for its ability to seal and protect furniture, but it also has many unheralded aesthetic benefits and possibilities. Waxes come in a variety of tones, but I primarily use clear or light beeswax-based antique waxes, sometimes paired with dark black waxes for accent color and age. You can mix pigments with clear wax to make your own colored waxes. You can even mix mica powders into your clear wax to make it shimmery and metallic.

FOR YOUR SAFETY: Waxes come in a solvent form, but are nontoxic, so you can use them indoors and without gloves.

FOR THE BEST RESULTS: Natural-bristle brushes are the best tool for applying waxes. Most waxes benefit from drying partially, until they are sticky (often called "coming to tack"), before you buff them to your desired sheen.

GILDING

Gilding is alchemy, and I'm passionate about that transformative process. It has been used for thousands of years, primarily as an accent. While this is most often how metallic leaf is still used today, you can gild an entire piece or surface for an indulgent effect. I'm very strategic about gilding and if I incorporate it, perhaps in a piece on which I'm doing a milk paint finish, I make sure to tone it down with steel wool so that I don't see pure, bright leaf. You'll probably have the most success beginning with gold leaf because, as a Dutch metal composition (rather than true gold), it's thicker and easier to hold and work with. As you get more practice, you might transition to trying rose gold or copper and, later, sterling silver, which requires a delicate hand.

FOR YOUR SAFETY: There are no special requirements when using metallic leaf; it is nontoxic and you don't need protective gloves.

FOR THE BEST RESULTS: Metallic leaf is delicate and it takes practice to master how to apply it smoothly. (You want to avoid touching the leaf itself except on the edge.) Apply gold leaf or other metallic leaf in a well-lit indoor space, away from breezes. This will allow you to spot any "holidays" (gaps) as well as to avoid having debris blown onto the surface of your piece, and it will give you more control over the fragile metallic leaf sheets. For much more information on gilding, see Gilding Like a Pro on page 49.

MIRROR

I've always loved antique mirrors, their age and patina. It never bothered me that I couldn't see well enough to do my lipstick in them! In addition to using them the traditional way, I love incorporating antique mirror on furniture (as a tabletop surface, for example, or as a sparkling accent), into an old frame, or even as a backsplash in the kitchen or bathroom. Antique and imperfect mirrors add a wonderful mixture of textures to a piece.

CREATE YOUR OWN SPRAY BOOTH
I often use what I call a spray booth or cardboard shadowbox to create a breeze-free scenario when I'm working outside. This way, there is both ventilation and protection from the wind and stray particles. All you need is a cardboard box that is bigger than the object or piece of furniture you're refinishing. For small pieces, it's usually easy to find a box that fits the bill. Cut out one of the four sides so that it is open. The other three sides and the top will protect your piece during the spraying and drying time. If you are working on a larger object or furnishing, you can duct-tape pieces of cardboard together to make a box with three sides, or you can buy large plastic sheets at the hardware store and hang them above the piece on three sides like drapes.

FOR YOUR SAFETY: The fumes and ingredients in the mirror stripping solution used in the antiquing process require taking precautions. Apply the solution only in a well-ventilated area and while wearing protective gloves that cover your wrists.

FOR THE BEST RESULTS: Using real mirror is important to achieve the desired antiqued effect in your refinishing projects. A few signs that your mirror is the real deal are that it has a dark gray backing and/or numbers. The backing of the mirror has been baked on, so it will respond the way we want when we treat it with a mirror stripping solution. The mirror should be American-made, as that will ensure it responds properly to both the stripping and antiquing solutions.

Warm weather helps activate the stripping solution more quickly. If you live in a climate that is warm year-round, you are all set. If you live in a climate that fluctuates, mirror antiquing projects are best done in warmer seasons. Either way, don't go overboard with the amount of stripping solution you apply; too much can actually prevent the mirror backing from activating and make it harder to remove it.

ZINC

Zincing is the process of taking shiny, galvanized sheet metal and transforming it to an aged, patinated finish that you can add to the top of a table, countertops, a backsplash, or premade galvanized-sheet-metal buckets, as you'll see in the André planters project on page 160. Zinc is a major element of the farmhouse look that has become so popular, which celebrates utility, texture, and history. Mixing zinc accents with your furniture, especially with milk paint or chalk-based finishes and waxes, will add subtle shine and strength.

FOR YOUR SAFETY: It's important to use protective gloves when working with zinc antiquing solution. Make sure they cover your wrists. There's no need to worry about fumes; you can use the solution indoors.

FOR THE BEST RESULTS: Galvanized metal is a good material to use with a zinc solution because it also contains a thin layer of zinc.

DRYING TIMES

The following drying times are approximate. Various factors such as the temperature and humidity where you live, the porousness of the surface you're refinishing, and how thickly you've applied the material can affect how long it takes. It's always better to err on the side of letting something dry longer if you have any doubts.

SOLUTION	DRYING TIME (APPROXIMATE)
Degreaser	20 minutes
Chalk-based (carbonate) paint	20 to 30 minutes per coat
Milk (casein) paint	20 to 30 minutes per coat
Spray lacquer	45 minutes to 1 hour per coat
Wax	15 to 30 minutes to come to tack (see page 25) and be ready for buffing
Gilding size	15 to 20 minutes to come to tack (see Gilding Like a Pro, page 49); will remain at tack for about 40 more minutes before drying completely

CHAPTER 4
CHALK-BASED PAINT

Chalk-based paint is calcium carbonate paint, but don't worry, we're not about to dive into a chemistry class. Calcium carbonate sounds very scientific, but the most important thing to know is that it's the main component of chalk. I love chalk-based paints not only because of the rich, matte finish they offer, but also because there's so much potential to build on them to create other amazing antiqued effects.

As you can imagine, paints started out very simply. Prehistoric humans used vegetables and clays and other items at close reach for color. Later, chalk and limestone and other sedimentary materials were ground up and added to paints for their durability. Chalk-based paints became widely popular in homes by the sixteenth and seventeenth centuries, and many vintage treasure hunters now covet the look they bestowed on antiques from the Victorian and Edwardian periods. In the twentieth century, as people began to demand durable, easy-to-scrub wall paints, the formula got more complicated. Chemicals were added. These chemicals can get in the way of the layered finishes we're trying to create, which is why it's always best to choose a natural chalk-based paint instead of a synthetic paint. The benefit of a natural chalk-based paint is that what you put on top of it, such as wax, will meld into it to create a beautiful layered finish. Of course, you can use calcium carbonate paint to instantly transform a piece of furniture and stop there (though I hope you will want to keep embellishing instead!). These painted surfaces also work like chalkboards, so they are fun on kitchen cabinets (where you can write and erase your weekly grocery list) and on walls (where you can show your guests the delicious dinner menu they're about to enjoy). Most exciting to me, though, is how chalk-based paints are such a versatile springboard—on surfaces ranging from a retro-chic midcentury modern stereo cabinet to a fabric pillow that would feel at home in the finest Venetian palazzo.

This 1960s vintage stereo cabinet, discovered at one of our favorite local shops, was no longer working, but it made a great console.

MIDCENTURY MODERN
In the mid-twentieth century, modern furniture design became popular, featuring clean lines (whether straight or curvy), graphic patterns, and bright colors. In recent years, midcentury modern styles came back on trend thanks to the influence of Mad Men; I think their simple silhouettes will always be prized, especially for imaginative refinishers.

THE ELTON STEREO CABINET

Vinyl has made a comeback, and vintage-furniture collectors like me could not be more thrilled. When you come across multifunctional pieces like this midcentury modern stereo cabinet, you know you have struck gold. How adorable is it that I also found a few retro records still tucked inside? A piece this classic and striking deserves to be given attention. Citron is my favorite bold hue, and it just so happened that my guest bedroom needed a beautiful, vibrant pop of color to anchor the dark gray walls. Gilded hardware takes it up another level. If you look beyond a piece's face value, a world of possibilities opens up.

MATERIALS

1 quart (960 ml) of citron chalk-based paint

1 booklet of gold leaf

One 8-ounce (240-ml) container of clear wax

Wood glue

Gilding size

Two 2-inch (5-cm) flat synthetic-bristle brushes

Round artist's brush (#12 or #14)

Small glue syringe

400 grit sandpaper

Painter's tape (optional)

2 clean, lint-free rags

Gentle degreaser

GETTING STARTED

WOOD DOCTOR *Vintage wood will often have rough or raised areas. Even though paint will adhere to the damage, your finish will appear uneven. Mend these damaged or buckling areas before you start. The better the prep work, the better the final results.*

Fill the syringe with wood glue and inject any raised or buckling areas of your wood or veneer projects. Set a pile of books on top of the mended area to flatten the glue beneath it during cure time. Let the glue dry overnight. After the glue has completely dried, sand the area smooth.

Many sixties-era stereos are no longer operational, but the cabinets have lots of decorative appeal. With a little paint and some decorative accents, you can turn a dud into a dream.

1

PREPPING THE SURFACE

Flea market finds and other antiques often have layers of grease or residue left over from years of wood treatments and conditioners, so we'll begin by cleaning all surfaces. You may find that some of the wood also needs a little repair to ensure a smooth surface for the paint. If the hardware is removable, take it out before you begin painting the piece (and give it a good scrub with the gentle degreaser); this will make the gilding process much easier.

1. Using a clean rag and a little degreaser, thoroughly wipe down your wood piece. Let the naturally porous wood dry completely for 10 to 20 minutes.

PAINTING THE WOOD

Chalk-based paint has the potential to provide an unbelievably smooth finish. If you run your hands across the entire project surface after each coat dries, you will catch any sneaky rough patches that can emerge.

2. Dip a flat synthetic brush into the chalk-based paint. Remove any excess by running the side of the brush along the lip of the container. Apply the paint to the wood in long, even strokes that overlap at the edges. Let the paint dry completely (about 20 to 30 minutes). Using the sandpaper, gently buff any rough areas, following the wood grain. Repeat the painting and sanding steps until the surface has an even, opaque finish. Most vintage wood will need three coats of paint to achieve full coverage.

GILDING THE HARDWARE

Outdated hardware often falls flat next to newly painted surfaces. Whether the hardware is stationary or removable, gold leaf has the power to transform even the homeliest elements. For more on gilding like a pro, see page 49.

3. If the hardware is stationary, dip the artist's brush into the gilding size and remove any excess. Apply it directly onto the hardware. You can also use painter's tape on the surrounding wood to ensure a clean-lined application. If it's removable hardware, be sure to gild its front, back (if it will be visible), and sides. After about 15 minutes, the size solution will turn from milky-white to clear. Test the size to see if it has come to tack by touching it with the tip of your ring finger; you're looking for a gentle pull.

4. Once this tack is evident, apply a trimmed-to-size sheet of gold leaf: Holding the gold leaf booklet taut at the folded portion of tissue paper near the spine on one side and at the other edge as shown, place the gold leaf against the surface and slowly pull away the single folded tissue sheet near the spine. (If you're gilding rounded hardware, you'll wrap an entire sheet of gold leaf around the perimeter of your handles.) Burnish the tissue paper side of the booklet by pressing with your fingertips in one direction to adhere the gold leaf sheet below to the size.

5. Gently pull the booklet away. Swipe away any loose gold leaf pieces with a clean flat brush.

WAXING THE CABINET

A layer of clear wax gives the naturally flat finish of the chalk-based paint a gentle sheen.

6 and 7. Using a little clear wax, apply it to the wooden surfaces of the cabinet with a clean rag. Let it dry (about 20 minutes), then buff to your desired sheen.

MIND THE GAPS *If you find any "holidays" (gaps) in gold leaf or paint coverage, it is best to start that section over: Re-gild the entire hardware piece rather than touching it up, or repaint the entire compromised section of painted wood. Seamless results will be worth the extra effort.*

THE GENEVIEVE DRESSER

Sometimes, if you get to the flea markets early, you can spot a find the second the dealer unloads her truck! That's just what happened with this exquisite dresser. I was awestruck the moment I saw it—by its size, its scale, the incredible knobs, and the painterly scrolls. If you find a piece like this, take some time to consider different finishing options, and be open to making adjustments after you start (sometimes the best ideas reveal themselves to you in midstream). I started out knowing I wanted to paint this dresser creamy white. The idea for adding the yellow details came later, as I realized they would create a sunny, friendly result. An all-over dark blue lacquer would have been an appealing alternative.

MATERIALS

1 quart (960 ml) of creamy-white chalk-based paint

1 quart (960 ml) of yellow chalk-based paint

1 can of light antique wax

1 can of dark antique wax

2-inch (5-cm) flat synthetic-bristle brush

Two 2-inch (5-cm) flat natural-bristle brushes

Round artist's brush (#12)

Painter's tape

Small square of cardboard

2 clean, lint-free rags

Gentle degreaser

GETTING STARTED

PREPPING THE SURFACE

1. Using a clean rag and a little degreaser, thoroughly scrub your wood piece. Let it dry completely for 10 to 20 minutes.

PAINTING THE DRESSER

As shown here, I painted the yellow details freehand (very carefully!). If you're fairly new to painting (or a little rusty), tape around the details after the white paint is dry to protect the creamy surfaces from stray yellow paint.

2. Dip the flat synthetic brush into the white paint. Remove any excess by running the side of your brush across the inner lip of the can. Paint the wood in long, even strokes that overlap at the edges. Let the paint dry completely (about 20 to 30 minutes).

3. Apply another coat and repeat until you reach your desired color and an even, opaque finish. Most vintage wood will need two or three coats of paint to achieve full coverage. Let the paint dry completely between each coat.

4 and 5. Dip an artist's brush into the yellow paint and remove any excess. Apply the paint to the ornamentation and the base. Let it dry completely. Apply a second coat of yellow paint. Let it dry completely. Remove the tape.

WAXING THE DRESSER

Light antique wax protects and seals the dresser. By adding dark wax "lowlights" to the piece as well, you are creating a subtle appearance of age. Apply wax to areas that might have been worn over time by people passing, hands pulling open the doors and drawers, and other serendipitous uses and accidents that add to the patina of a well-loved and well-preserved piece.

6. Dip a clean flat natural-bristle brush into the light antique wax. Remove any excess by running the side of the brush along the piece of cardboard. Brush the wax over the entire piece so that you have full, even coverage. Let it dry for 10 to 15 minutes, then test the wax to see if it has come to tack by touching it with the tip of your ring finger; you're looking for a gentle pull.

7 and 8. Once the light antique wax has come to tack, dip a clean flat natural-bristle brush into the dark antique wax. Remove any excess. Brush the dark wax over areas of the piece that might look worn, such as the ornamentation. Apply the dark wax to about 20 percent of the piece for a realistic appearance of age. Let the dark wax dry for 30 minutes or until it comes to tack. Using a clean rag, buff the newly waxed areas to your desired sheen.

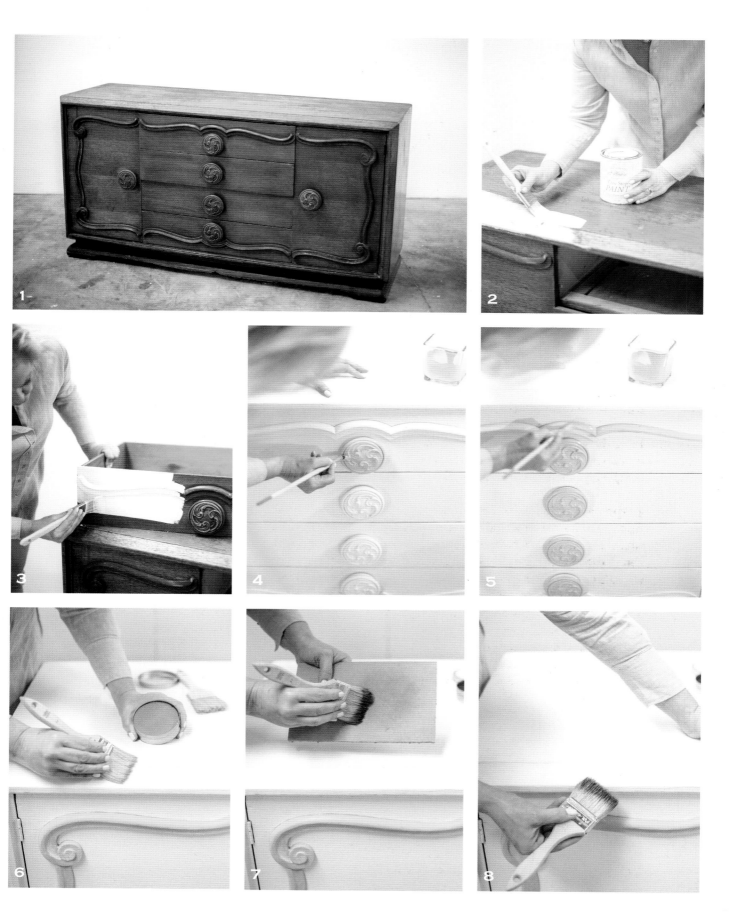

These lovely accent pillows are made from Fortuny fabric. The following project was inspired by this look.

THE SOFIA PILLOW

This design was inspired by Fortuny, a Spanish artist and fashion and product designer known for creating gorgeous, innovative fabrics and spinning them into some of the most desirable confections in Venice (where he was based), Paris, and other centers of style. This pillow will be a true object of desire in your home. (You might want to make several!) And, of course, you can use this technique to create striking fabric for other purposes, like napkins and tablecloths or even framed like art. In the project shown, I've dyed two matching squares of fabric separately so that the pillow has the golden design on each side, created with mica powder; you could also dye an already-sewn pillow cover and create this design on one side, then just paint the other side of the cover a solid color with a chalk-based paint.

STENCIL OPTIONS *It's ideal to use a large adhesive stencil that is roughly the size of your pillow so that you don't have to move it around or worry about trying to line up the edges. You might consider buying an adhesive wall stencil and then cutting it down to size for your pillow. There are many different kinds of adhesive stencils available online; if you want to make your own pattern instead, you can do so using contact paper, which is available at many hardware and home stores and some grocery stores. Using the grid on the back of the contact paper as a guide, draw your desired pattern. Cut it out with a fine craft blade and attach the adhesive side of the stencil to your pillow before applying the mica glaze. If you'd like to use a nonadhesive stencil, be sure to choose one made of a thick mylar or other material that can hold up to being taped to your fabric, wiped off, and reused multiple times.*

MATERIALS

1 pint (480 ml) of light green chalk-based paint (about 6 ounces [180 ml] needed)

1 pint (480 ml) of medium green chalk-based paint (about 6 ounces [180 ml] needed)

1 pint (480 ml) of dark green chalk-based paint (about 6 ounces [180 ml] needed)

2 matching squares of white or cream 100-percent-cotton fabric at your desired pillow size, including seam allowances (the finished pillow shown is 19 inches [48 cm] square; if yours is smaller, scale down your materials amounts accordingly)

One 1-quart (960-ml) can of clear water- or oil-based glaze (about 2 tablespoons [30 ml] needed for 2 pieces of fabric)

One 4-ounce (120-ml) jar of gold mica powder (about 2 tablespoons [30 ml] needed for 2 pieces of fabric)

One 12- to 16-ounce (360- to 480-ml) bottle of squeezable liquid natural beeswax (about 3 ounces [90 ml] needed for 2 pieces of fabric)

Adhesive stencil (see sidebar)

4 natural sea wool sponges

Protective gloves

2 small squares of cardboard

Plastic spoons or stirring sticks

Plastic putty knife

2 or more clean, lint-free rags

Small glass or plastic container

Large plastic container

2 disposable plastic cups

THE SHIMMER OF MICA *Mica is a mineral that is found in nature in sheets, and has been used in powder form for ornamentation for hundreds of years. It is available in gold, silver, copper, and other metallic colors. You can use it as a pigment and mix it into a glaze, as we do here, or into a wax when you want to add a luxurious accent to your decor.*

Luxury doesn't have to be expensive—and you get all the bragging rights if you create it yourself.

GETTING STARTED

PREPPING THE SURFACE

Make sure your pillow cover or fabric is clean of all dust and dirt. In the following steps, you will be diluting the chalk-based paint with water; if you like, you can do this for all three paints before you begin. Be sure to stir them until smooth just before use.

DYEING AND MOTTLING THE FABRIC

The first step is to create a tie-dyed effect using a light, medium, and dark paint in the same family. Feel free to substitute your favorite colors for the colors shown. You'll want to wear gloves while dyeing the fabric. I recommend working with only one piece of fabric at a time because you want the three different colors to blend a little to create an organic look. It's important *not* to let the fabric dry completely between steps; you'll be sponging on the second and third colors while the first is still wet.

1. In the large plastic container, dilute ½ cup (120 ml) of light green paint with 1 to 1½ cups (240 to 360 ml) of warm tap water (2 to 3 parts warm tap water for every 1 part paint). The diluted paint should be the consistency of milk.

2. Holding one piece of fabric on opposite edges, gather it into your hands in an accordion shape.

3. Press it into the light green paint solution and move it around until it gets fully saturated, while keeping it folded.

4. Wring out the excess paint. There will be some negative space without paint where the folds were.

5. Lay the fabric flat and let it partially dry (about 15 to 20 minutes) in a well-ventilated room.

6. In a plastic cup, dilute ½ cup (120 ml) of the medium green paint with 1 to 1½ cups (240 to 360 ml) of warm tap water. In a

separate plastic cup, dilute the dark green paint the same way.

7. Dip one of the clean sponges into the medium green paint. Remove any excess by squeezing it onto a piece of cardboard. The sponge should be wet but not soaked with paint.

8 and 9. While the light green paint is still partially wet, drip and sponge the medium green paint onto the fabric in the areas of negative space where the folds kept paint from being absorbed. The light and medium green paints will partially blend; don't worry if you're not precise since the randomness of the melding adds to the beauty. While the light and medium green paints are still partially wet, repeat step 3 with the dark paint, this time dripping and sponging it on in an organic, mottled pattern, covering about one-third of the fabric so that the light and medium green show through everywhere else. Repeat steps 1 to 10 with the second piece of fabric. Let both pieces of fabric dry completely, ideally overnight.

CREATING THE GILDED PATTERN

Once your fabric is completely dry, I recommend that you iron it so that you have a smooth surface for the stencil to adhere to.

10. Remove the backing from the adhesive stencil.

11. Apply the adhesive side to the fabric.

12. Using a plastic putty knife, burnish the back side of the stencil by pressing firmly in smooth strokes in one direction so that it adheres to the fabric.

13. Remove the masking film from the stencil.

14 and 15. In a small container, pour 1 tablespoon (15 ml) of glaze into 1 tablespoon (15 ml) of gold mica powder and mix well with a plastic spoon.

16. Dip a clean sponge into the mica solution and remove any excess. Press the sponge down randomly over the back of the stencil to create a mottled effect on the exposed fabric. Be sure to get enough coverage so that the pattern of the stencil forms, but with some natural-looking gaps and lighter patches in the gilded parts so they look handmade and as if they have aged. Repeat steps 12 to 17 with the second piece of fabric. Let the fabric dry completely (about 45 minutes).

17. Carefully remove the stencil from the fabric.

18. Squeeze some of the liquid beeswax onto a clean rag. Rub the wax over the entire fabric surface. Repeat on the second piece of fabric. After 15 to 20 minutes, test the wax to see if it has come to tack by touching it with the tip of your ring finger; you're looking for a gentle pull. Once the wax has come to tack, use a clean rag to buff the waxed pieces of fabric.

SOFTENING AND PROTECTING THE FABRIC

Paints typically add stiffness to the fabric. Applying a coat of wax after the dyeing process makes the fabric softer and more supple. It also protects the fabric from wine stains and other damage, and makes it easy to wipe clean.

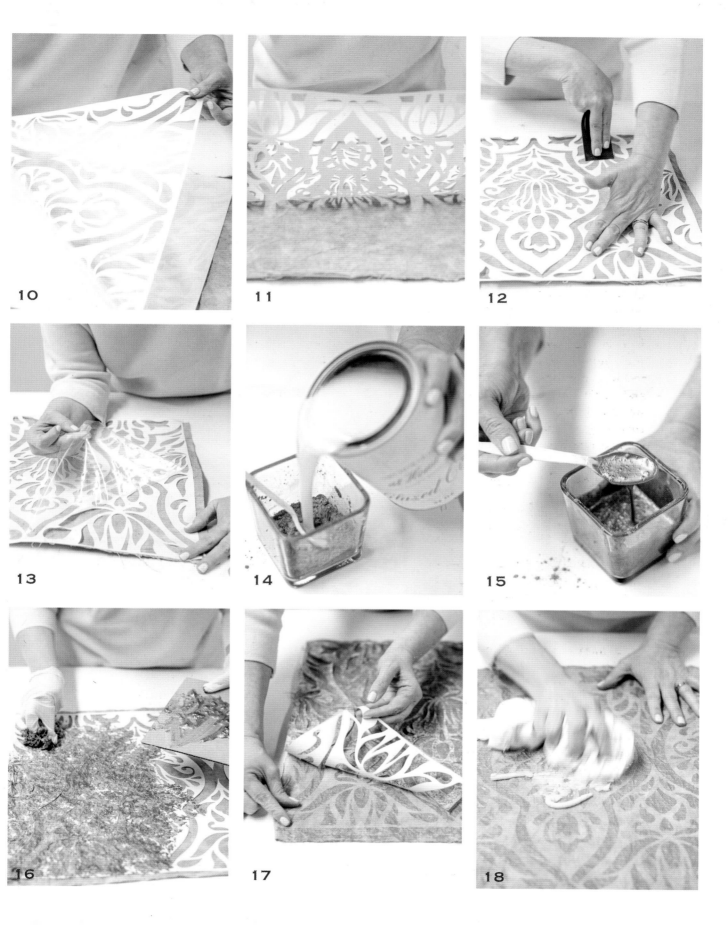

CHAPTER 5
GILDING

The art of gilding dates back thousands of years. In the earliest uses of the technique, Egyptian royalty had large gold nuggets pounded and then cut into small slivers to adorn their palaces, possessions, and sarcophagi, hoping to fool the eye into thinking their compositions were solid gold. As civilizations evolved, so did the uses of gold leaf. In first-century Roman architecture, gold leaf was a sign of prestige. Stately columns, friezes, statues, and even lampposts were adorned with gold. Later, artists adopted the skill and gilded ceilings, altar sticks, cherubs, angelic wings, and putti. Adorning massive cathedrals became many artists' main line of expertise, fame, and income.

Today, gilding is everywhere. Picture frames, furniture, book bindings, and even artisanal food are embellished with gold leaf. While 24-karat gold is still used occasionally, the majority of "gold" leaf used in decor today is actually a thin colored Dutch metal. There are many reasons that the use of faux gilding better serves our everyday modern uses, two of which are cost and ease of application.

Most gilding—even faux—is saved for accenting carvings and hardware. Rarely would you want to apply gold leaf to an entire piece of furniture.

All of the applications in the projects that follow use gold leaf and glue that you can easily find online or at craft stores. Most gold leaf is sold in a book of 25 sheets (and this is usually more than enough for the projects in the book or any other gilding projects you might undertake). Each gold leaf sheet is separated from the next by a protective layer of tissue paper. I like to work with a medium-sized booklet, no bigger than a hand, and trim the booklet down into smaller pieces as I go. The other product you will need is a glue called size. This isn't just any household or school glue, though. Size is specially formulated not only to adhere to just about any surface you can imagine, but also to dry to a sticky "tack" for easy attachment (think of the adhesive on the back of sticky notes).

I enjoy collections because the repetition is pleasing. These objects from my collection of gold wreaths are a great example of gilding.

GILDING LIKE A PRO

SIZE

You'll want to apply size with a long, slender artist's brush. Tapered bristles will serve you best because many of your accent surfaces will have crevices and narrow edges. Brush a full-coverage coat of size over the entire area you wish to gild. Size goes on white and milky so that you can see where you've applied it. Sometimes you have to look closely to make sure you have full coverage. If you find a spot you missed, you have come across what is called a "holiday." This is not the same as a vacation! This art term refers to gaps in application. Wherever there is a "holiday" in your size, there will be a "holiday" in your gilding results. It is very important to fix these sneaky breaks in coverage before adding gold leaf.

How plain would this painted chair be without the gold leaf accents? The shimmer makes all the difference.

TACK

In order for gold leaf to properly adhere to a surface, the size you've applied must come to "tack," a semidry, sticky form. If you apply the gold leaf before the size comes to tack, the result will be a swimming mess that never dries. Here's how to verify that your size has come to tack: Once you have established full size coverage over the intended surface, wait about 15 minutes for the size to turn clear and shiny, then lightly touch the surface with your ring finger. (The weakest of fingers provides the perfect pressure to feel for pullback without disturbing the seamless application of the glue.) If the size tugs or pulls against your skin a little, it has reached tack. In most climates, this takes about 15 minutes and the size will remain tacky for about 45 more minutes (in other words, about an hour after application), but I always recommend using the ring finger test to be certain.

Gilding has been used for several millennia to enhance the value of objects and surfaces and to symbolize the owner's wealth.

TRIMMING GOLD LEAF

Gold-leaf booklets are held together with a spine just like other books. Since most project surfaces (such as hardware) will be smaller than the leaf sheet of a medium-sized booklet, I recommend that, before you begin, trim your booklet down to a size that fits your project. Trim the entire book each time, not just a few sheets.

Let's say you are gilding three 1½-inch (4-cm) pulls on a dresser. Hold the spine of the booklet while trimming the entire leaf booklet to about 2½ inches (6.5 cm). Don't trim the leaf too far; you'll want to leave a bit of a margin to allow for a small overlap on either side.

APPLYING GOLD LEAF

Avoid touching gold leaf with your bare fingers. The thin sheets are extremely delicate and will easily break if handled. When you are ready to apply the leaf, fold back the protective tissue paper of your trimmed booklet to reveal the gold leaf. This will create a folded area of tissue paper near the spine. Hold this folded area between one index finger and thumb. Hold the other end of the booklet between your other index finger and thumb (you will be touching the edge of the top piece of gold leaf). Stretching the booklet to a smooth, tight tension, place the sheet directly over the surface that's come to tack.

Hold the booklet in place with one hand and pull the folded single sheet of tissue paper off of the booklet. Still holding the gold-leaf sheet in place with one hand, use the other hand to brush the tissue paper side of the booklet with firm, one-direction strokes. This repetitive left-to-right pressure is called "burnishing." The firmer and more thoroughly you burnish, the more seamlessly and solidly your gold leaf will attach. Once you have burnished the entire application area, pull the booklet away to reveal the attached gold leaf.

FINISHING

Your newly gilded area will always have loose flakes around it that need to be removed. Never brush away these bits of leaf with your fingers; instead, use a clean brush such as a chip brush, which is flat and made of soft, natural bristles that are perfect for delicate jobs like this. Use it in a gentle, one-direction stroking motion to brush away any lingering loose flakes and reveal the clean gold-leaf application.

TROUBLESHOOTING

If you find any "holidays" (gaps) in your final product, do not fret. It is always better to start the process over instead of trying to patch in gold leaf. Size will adhere to any surface, even gold leaf. Simply start at step 1 (applying the size) and try again!

Don't sneeze! Gold leaf is very thin, and as light as butterfly wings!

Gilded objects transform a tabletop; although small, they make a bold statement.

Gold over metal (known as "ormolu") adorns this curtain tieback and accent table (opposite, top left and bottom right), offering a slightly different kind of shine from gold-leaf accents over wood (top right and bottom left).

THE NICOLAS NIGHTSTAND

I popped into my favorite local antiques market, where they know me very well, to see if I could find a small chest for my guest bedroom. The minute my eyes caught this sleek dresser, I knew it fit the bill, though it has no pedigree. When the dealer gave me a $25 quote, I snatched up this solid wood beauty and headed for the workshop. I will admit, when I purchased this chest, I had no idea what finish I would use, but as soon as I saw it against my wild floral wallpaper, I knew a bold blue color accented with gold leaf would showcase the traditional lines I loved so much.

MATERIALS

1 quart (960 ml) of blue chalk-based paint
1 bottle of white cerusing wax
1 booklet of gold-leaf sheets
Gilding size
2-inch (5-cm) flat synthetic-bristle brush
2-inch (5-cm) flat natural-bristle brush
Round artist's brush (#12 or #14)
2 clean, lint-free rags
Gentle degreaser
Painter's tape
1 pad of #0000 steel wool
Small square of cardboard

GETTING STARTED

Over the lifetime of all furnishings, a stubborn layer of grime builds up from use. It's important to remove all grease that can act as a surfactant before beginning to ensure a clean, smooth surface. If your wooden piece has scratches or other areas that might prevent a smooth finish, you can use wood glue to repair them (see Wood Doctor, page 31).

1. Using a clean rag and a little degreaser, thoroughly scrub the surfaces of the dresser.

2. Remove and clean all hardware. If there is extensive grime buildup, I usually soak the hardware in a diluted degreaser for a few hours.

PAINTING THE DRESSER

Complete painting one section of the dresser at a time. First paint the top to completion, then one side, then the other, and, last, paint the front. If there are drawers to be painted, take them out of the dresser before you begin painting and lay them flat on the ground to prevent sagging. For best results, paint several thin, even coats and let dry completely between coats.

3. Hold a flat brush in your hand as you would a pen. Dip the tip of your brush directly into the can of paint. Remove any excess paint by running the side of the brush across the inner lip of the can. Start in the corner of the surface and brush the paint to a midway point, using long, even strokes and being careful to overlap the edges of each stroke. Reload the brush with paint and brush it to a midway point from the other side. Let each coat dry completely (about 20 to 30 minutes). Repeat until the piece has an opaque, even finish. Most wooden furniture will need three layers of paint to achieve full coverage.

THIN, EVEN COATS *Chalk-based paints have been known to crack if the initial application is too thick or subsequent layers are applied too soon.*

When refinishing a piece of furniture worth cherishing, think of your paint color as a jumping-off point toward breathtaking results, rather than the final outcome.

GILDING THE HARDWARE

Gilding the hardware and the drawer edges of simple furnishings like this dresser not only adds warmth and glamour, but also showcases the accents and carvings. All of the raised areas that make up the framework of a piece and the hardware are perfect to gild. You might need to use painter's tape around some trim and accents before applying size to ensure a clean line of gold leaf is achieved.

4. Dip the tip of the artist's brush into the gilding size and remove any excess. Apply a full-coverage layer of size in long, even strokes. When working with rounded hardware, be sure to cover the entire surface in size. After about 15 minutes, the size solution will turn from milky-white to clear. Test the size to see if it has come to tack by touching it with the tip of your ring finger; you're looking for a gentle pull.

5, 6, and 7. Once this tack is evident, apply a trimmed-to-size sheet of gold leaf: Holding the gold-leaf booklet taut at the folded portion of tissue paper near the spine on one side and at the other edge as shown, place the gold leaf against the surface and slowly pull away the single folded tissue sheet near the spine. (If you're gilding rounded hardware, you'll wrap an entire sheet of gold leaf around the perimeter of your handles.) Burnish the tissue paper side of the booklet by pressing with your fingertips in one direction to adhere the gold-leaf sheet below to the size, and pull the booklet away.

8. Let the size dry completely (about an hour after you applied it). Gently swipe away any loose shards of gold leaf with a clean flat brush. Repeat steps 4 through 8 on all desired areas of the furniture. Let the drawer trim dry completely (at least an hour).

9. If you want a duller shine, gently run #0000 steel wool along the length of the gilded surface in one direction.

WAXING THE DRESSER

At the very last minute, I decided that my bold blue chest would look stunning under a cloudy layer of soft cerusing wax. Sparks of creativity are what I love most about the restoration journey; embrace them when they come.

10. Dip the tip of a clean flat brush into the cerusing wax. Remove any excess wax by swiping the bristles over the square of cardboard.

11. Brush the wax over the furniture surface in long, even strokes. Let it come to tack (about 15 to 20 minutes).

12. Using a clean rag and working from left to right, buff the entire waxed surface to a subtle sheen. The more you buff, the glossier the sheen will become.

A pair of twin headboards, possibly from the late 1800s, features gold leaf on the raised trim and carvings.

Black or gray and gold look gorgeous together, as on this geometric-patterned armoire (opposite) and decorative stool. The Hugo table (following spread) benefits from the same color scheme.

THE HUGO TABLE

If you're like me, you can always find a use for more small side tables—when guests come for cocktails, as a perch for books you're reading (or hope to find time for soon), and as a spot for the remote (so you never have to search). When I saw this adorable iron table base at an open-air flea market—a find at just a few dollars—I thought its lovely, slender legs would look perfect placed beside my beloved Eames lounge chair. To create a fitted tabletop, I needed to have a piece of wood cut to size first. Then I needed to devise a finish swanky enough to complement the midcentury modern vibe, yet versatile enough to travel from room to room during party season. Since stone finishes will always be on trend, I thought a gilded tiger's-eye finish would be perfect. The clean lines of the iron base paired with a natural stone pattern turn this into a functional art piece. This project combines multiple techniques and materials, so it's a great one when you're feeling like you have the time and moxie.

MATERIALS

1 quart (960 ml) of black chalk-based paint

1 can of black spray lacquer

1 can of clear high-gloss spray lacquer

1 bottle of water-based glaze

1 booklet of gold-leaf sheets

Three 3-inch (7.5-cm) foam brushes

2 round artist's brushes (#12 or #14)

2-inch (5-cm) flat natural-bristle brush

Wood piece for the tabletop, cut to size

Masking tape

Fine craft knife

Art eraser

2 clean, lint-free rags

Gentle degreaser

Small disposable container

GETTING STARTED

PREPPING THE SURFACE

Many vintage iron elements have a greasy residue that was applied to protect against rust and oxidation. Before you begin, remove this stubborn surfactant using a clean rag and a little degreaser to scrub the table base thoroughly. Both chalk-based paint and glaze are free of dangerous chemical fumes and can be used indoors—just make sure to protect the surfaces around your work area. The spray lacquer does have fumes, so apply it in a well-ventilated (breeze-free) outdoor area. I recommend that you mix the custom pigmented glaze described in step 11 during the drying time of the gold leaf in step 9. You might also want to make the art eraser tool described in step 11 before you start.

PAINTING THE BASE AND TOP

When creating a brand-new composition by pairing new and old elements, it is important for the end result to appear as though these elements had always belonged together. Using a connecting color or design element will unify your resourceful creation, as the play of black and gold does here. The chalk-based paint offers the perfect protective coat for the iron base, but the gilding requires a brushstroke-free, less absorbent surface, which is why I chose spray lacquer for the top. It's best to pick similar spray lacquer and chalk-based paint colors that complement each other, although you may want a darker hue for the iron base.

1. Dip the tip of the foam brush directly into the paint. Remove any excess paint by running the side of the brush across the inner lip of the container. Paint the entire iron table base using light, even strokes and being careful to overlap the edges of each stroke. Let the paint dry completely (about 20 to 30 minutes).

GO WIDE *A wide foam brush is the perfect tool for small surfaces needing a very smooth finish.*

2. While the iron base is drying, lacquer the tabletop. Hold the aerosol spray can 10 to 12 inches (25 to 30.5 cm) away from the surface of your tabletop and spray in short, even bursts, working your way from the top corner to the bottom until the entire surface has been spray painted. Let it dry completely (about 45 minutes to 1 hour). Repeat until both the base and tabletop have an even, opaque finish. Most surfaces will need two or three coats to achieve full coverage.

GILDING THE BASE

Applying a small amount of gold leaf to the base will draw attention to the table legs and integrate nicely with the finish on the tabletop.

3. After the paint on the base is dry, use masking tape to mark the table legs about 1½ inches (4 cm) up from the feet; this is the area to be gilded.

4. Dip the tip of a round artist's brush into the gilding size and remove any excess. Apply a full-coverage layer of size around the entire perimeter of the 1½-inch (4-cm) section in

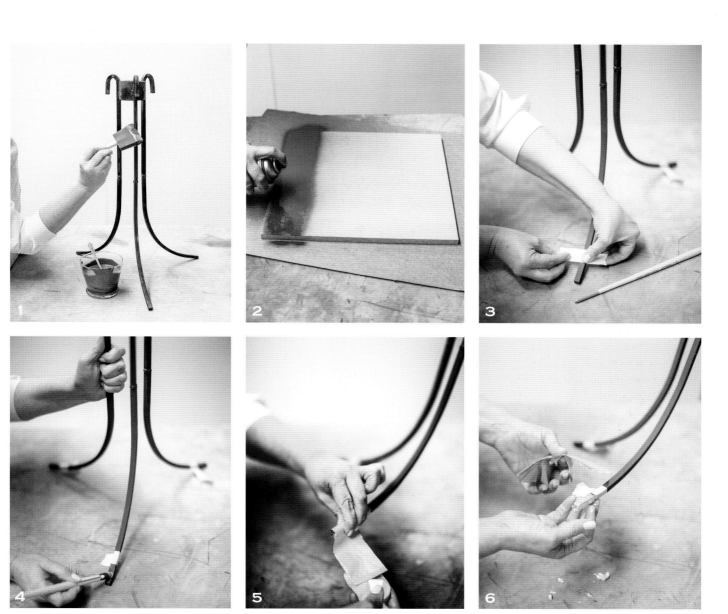

long, even strokes. After about 15 minutes, the size solution will turn from milky-white to clear. Test the size to see if it has come to tack by touching it with the tip of your ring finger; you're looking for a gentle pull.

5. Holding the gold-leaf booklet taut at the folded portion of tissue paper near the spine on one side and at the other edge as shown, wrap the entire booklet over the size and around the perimeter of the foot tip. Slowly pull away the single folded tissue sheet near the spine.

6. Burnish the tissue paper side of the booklet by pressing with your fingertips in one direction to adhere the gold-leaf sheet below to the size, and pull the booklet away. Let the size dry completely (about an hour after you applied it). Gently swipe away any loose shards of gold leaf with a clean flat brush.

GILDING THE TOP

In order to create the tiger's-eye effect on the tabletop, you will first cover it with a gold-leaf base, which later gets partially revealed through the pigmented glaze.

7. Dip the tip of a clean artist's brush into gilding size and remove any excess. Apply a full-coverage layer of size to the entire tabletop. Let the size come to tack (about 15 minutes).

8. Begin at the top left corner and apply entire sheets of gold leaf to the tabletop using the same application techniques you followed for the table base. Overlap the edges of each sheet at least half an inch to ensure full coverage.

9. Continue until the entire surface has been gilded. The size will remain at tack for about an hour, but you'll want to work as quickly as possible to make sure the application is seamless. Let the size dry completely and gently swipe away any loose shards of gold leaf with a clean flat brush.

CREATING THE TIGER'S-EYE FINISH

To create the faux tiger's-eye finish, you will first need to make a simple comb tool by carving an artist's eraser. The grooves you cut into it will pull up some of the glaze, creating a random, natural-looking pattern like the striations in a stone. This homemade tool can be washed and reused countless times, and you can use it to create many different faux stone effects, including malachite, lapis lazuli, and sardonyx stones. This eraser tool is more fun and less complicated to use than the combing tools you can buy.

10. Using a fine craft knife, slice ¼-inch- (6-mm-) long grooves into each side of the eraser, being careful to cut away from yourself. Feel free to space the grooves randomly and to cut some of them deeper than others; they should be close together, like teeth in a comb, but completely uneven and asymmetrical.

11. In a disposable container, mix 1 part chalk-based paint, 1 part glaze, and 1 part water (¼ cup [60 ml] of each) to create a custom pigmented glaze. Stir until completely smooth. Dip a clean foam brush into the glaze and remove any excess. Apply the semitransparent glaze over the gilded tabletop in long, even strokes, being careful to overlap the edges of each stroke.

12. While the glaze is still wet, create the tiger's-eye effect: Hold the art eraser tool between your ring finger and thumb at a 45-degree angle and, starting from the top left corner of the tabletop, graze the wet surface from top to bottom in a single continuous pass, gently pivoting your wrist now and then to create striations. (It helps to consult a picture of tiger's-eye so that you can mimic the stone's natural foliation.) Repeat, overlapping the edges of each pass as shown, until you have covered the entire tabletop.

13. Let the glaze dry completely (about 2 to 3 hours). While this drying time passes, prepare the finishing glaze by mixing 1 more part water into the remaining custom pigmented glaze from step 12. (For example, if you are left with ½ cup [120 ml] of pigmented glaze, add an additional ¼ cup [60 ml] of water to thin it.) Once the tiger's-eye finish has fully dried, apply a layer of finishing glaze to the entire tabletop with a clean foam brush.

14. Immediately after applying the glaze, create a pad with a lint-free rag and finesse and soften your finish by patting the pad into the wet transparent glaze. Let it dry completely overnight.

EASY REDO *If you aren't satisfied with the initial striation pattern you made with your eraser tool, simply wipe away the glaze and start the process over. It might take a few tries in the beginning, but confidence in your final product is most important!*

FINISHING THE TABLETOP

Using clear, high-gloss lacquer seals the tabletop for functionality with a hint of beautiful shine.

15. Once the tabletop is dry, apply a full-coverage layer of a clear high-gloss lacquer, holding the spray can 10 to 12 inches (25 to 30.5 cm) from the surface and spraying in short, even strokes over the top and sides until they are completely covered. Let the lacquer dry completely (about 45 minutes to 1 hour). Attach the top to the base.

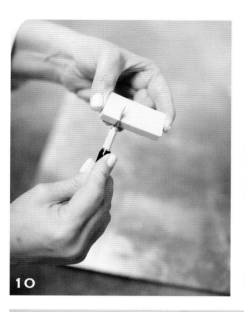

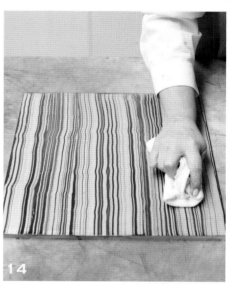

CHAPTER 6

LACQUER

If fruit is nature's candy, then lacquer is nature's plastic. A highly desirable finish thanks to its shine and its resilience to water and heat, lacquer has been used for thousands of years as a luxurious coating and decorative material, from elaborately carved furniture in the palaces of Chinese emperors to the finest cars in the world, which in the mid-twentieth century sometimes received twenty or more coats of lacquer.

Today, of course, we want the high gloss and depth of lacquer without so much fuss. The lacquers available today often require

Lacquer originated from the "lac," an insect that creates a secretion rich in shellac. It originated in Asia and dates back thousands of years. Charcoal or iron oxides were mixed in to create colors.

applying only two or three coats to an object or a piece of furniture. With a similar makeup to nail polish (and thus, similar challenges), these lacquers still require more elbow grease than chalk-based or milk paints because of how revealing a medium lacquer is. Any imperfections show through in the final result, so it's key to start with a completely clean and smooth surface, and to let each layer of lacquer dry and then sand it to remove any bumps or particles before applying the next coat. Unlike most paints, with each layer sitting on top of the next to create an opaque finish, layers of lacquer meld together, refracting light and assuming a wonderful sense of depth and shine, which shifts in an eye-catching way depending on where you're standing.

Your efforts will be worth it: Lacquered pieces are in demand not only because of their individual appeal, but also because they offer an irresistible modern mix with other decorating elements including matte painted items, mirrors, soft rugs, and bold art. And there's no need to limit yourself to lacquering large pieces of wood furniture, either: I love this finish on appliances, found objects, glass tables, even lamps—as you'll see in the pages to follow.

Thanks to vivid red lacquer, this Georgian-style pediment mirror frame looks edgy in all the right ways.

THE AUGUSTUS LAMP

One of my favorite corners in our home has the perfect juxtaposition of design: a welcoming Egg chair, a pretty side table, and crisp white moldings. Unfortunately, though, it was just too dark for reading and drinking a cup of tea or doing any of the activities we would otherwise love to enjoy there. Every off-the-shelf lamp I tried got lost beside the sheer girth of my dark gray Egg chair. I soon realized that the retro charm my anchor pieces were demanding could not be found in a designer boutique; I needed to go antiquing. Lo and behold, the perfect lamp and shade were waiting for me as soon as I walked into my trusty flea market. The slender body and wide shade of this 1970s accent definitely complemented my retro vibe, and now that the amber body has been lacquered and the dingy shade fabric replaced with a much more fun treatment, the lamp lights up this corner—literally. You can create the same result on a new, store-bought lamp using the same techniques I detail in this project: lacquering the body of the lamp, then painting the shade with stripes.

MATERIALS

1 can of white spray lacquer

1 quart (960 ml) of white chalk-based paint (about 8 ounces [240 ml] needed)

1 quart (960 ml) of blue chalk-based paint (about 4 ounces [120 ml] needed)

Two 2-inch (5-cm) flat synthetic-bristle brushes

Painter's tape

#2 pencil

Clean, lint-free rag

Gentle degreaser

Small washable container

GETTING STARTED

PREPPING THE SURFACE

When you are lacquering a piece, you'll get the best results if the surface is clean and even. Vintage finds often have a buildup of dirt or grease that you'll want to remove so you can start with a smooth surface, and even new, store-bought lamps can have chemicals or dust or fingerprints from handling.

1 and 2. Using the clean rag and degreaser, thoroughly scrub the lamp, any metal accents, and the fabric shade. Apply painter's tape over the metal elements and electrical components.

SET THE STAGE Tackle your projects in stages rather than regretting a move made too soon. Timeless metal accents, like the brass base and top on this lamp, are sometimes the icing on the cake. You can always come back and paint or gild them later.

LACQUERING THE LAMP

You can never go wrong with a light-colored lacquer. Not only does it give dark and dated surfaces a fresh start, but it also heightens the clean, glossy shine. While chalk-based paint can be applied indoors, spray lacquer needs to be applied in a well-ventilated area, far from unpredictable breezes. I recommend having a cardboard shadowbox (see Create Your Own Spray Booth, page 26) on hand to save you from unnecessary headaches and heartaches when painting outdoors.

3. Holding the spray can 10 inches (25 cm) from the lamp body, spray the lacquer in long, even strokes, being careful to overlap the edges as you move across the surface. To avoid undesirable drips, do not linger in one area too long. Most glass surfaces need two coats of lacquer for an opaque finish. Let each coat dry completely (about 45 minutes to 1 hour) before adding the next. (Note: Unlike wood and other surfaces, you shouldn't sand glass surfaces between coats of lacquer.)

PAINTING THE SHADE

Most vintage lamp shades are dingy and cannot be used as is. If you dilute chalk-based paint with 30 percent warm tap water (for example, 2 ounces [60 ml] of warm tap water for every 7 ounces [210 ml] of paint), you can transform any outdated lamp shade your heart desires. (The dilution ensures that even after a few coats, the paint will be thin enough that light will still filter through the finished shade.) Before you apply the painter's tape directly over the newly painted fabric, a 24-hour dry time is recommended to prevent peeling.

4. In the washable container, dilute the chalk-based paint with warm tap water. Use a clean brush to apply a full-coverage layer of the diluted paint over the entire fabric shade. Dip the brush into the paint and remove any excess by running the side of the brush across the inner lip of the container. Most fabric shades need at least two coats of paint to achieve full coverage; however, varying colors and textile types will have the ultimate say. Allow the first (and, if applicable, second)

coat to dry for up to 24 hours to prevent the painter's tape from pulling the new paint off in the following steps.

5. After the base coat(s) has dried, measure out three even sections for the striped pattern, using a #2 pencil to trace guidelines around the shade. Apply painter's tape between them as shown.

6. Using a clean brush, apply a full-strength coat of blue chalk-based paint to create the stripes. Let it dry completely (at least 24 hours). Once the darker coat of paint has dried, slowly remove the painter's tape for the big reveal.

THE DONOVAN CHAIRS

I must confess that I have a bit of a chair fetish. From side chairs to dining chairs, corner chairs to entryway chairs, every room in my home always needs an extra chair! Dressers and tables are a dime a dozen, but an easy-to-refinish chair can be hard to find. If you ever come across an adorable duo like my new vinyl friends, you must snatch them up instantly. The nailhead trim and faux bamboo adorning my new side chairs offered the perfect complements to my favorite but lonely Hollywood Regency console. I loved the idea of keeping the mood light in my upstairs landing and decided to use a soft yet memorable blue for the chair cushions. You may be surprised to know that you can paint vinyl and some fairly smooth fabrics like linen or cotton; this project shows you how. The layer of clear wax repels stains and helps preserve the painted vinyl color. See Chapter 3, page 25 for more on using waxes.

MATERIALS

1 quart (960 ml) of soft blue chalk-based paint

1 can of white spray lacquer

1 container of clear wax

2-inch (5-cm) flat synthetic-bristle brush

Masking or painter's tape

400 grit sandpaper

Kraft paper

2 clean, lint-free rags

Gentle degreaser

Small washable container

GETTING STARTED

PREPPING THE SURFACE

Even though this project, like many others, will be done in separate phases, go ahead and clean the entire body of both chairs to expedite the process. Given that these chairs remain identical twins, restoring them in tandem will make your job much easier. Before you begin, you'll want to clean off any surfactants.

1. Using the clean rag and a little degreaser, thoroughly scrub each chair.

2. Apply masking or painter's tape around all wood areas bordering the vinyl upholstery.

PAINTING THE VINYL

Diluting your paint is key to smooth results on all types of upholstery. Here, we are applying the chalk-based paint with a brush, but we would also dilute it for use in an airless sprayer, which is another tool I love for applying paints in a clean, even fashion (though these sprayers are an investment!). The painted vinyl gets protection from a coat of clear wax.

3. In the washable container, dilute the chalk-based paint with 20 percent warm tap water (for example, you would use 3.2 ounces [100 ml] of tap water for every 16 ounces [480 ml] of paint). Dip the brush into the paint and remove any excess by running the side of the brush across the inner lip of the container. Paint each seat cushion in long, even strokes until both have a good base coat. Let the paint dry completely (at least 30 minutes) before sanding or applying the next coat.

4. Once the paint is dry, sand the vinyl gently to remove any bumps. Repeat steps 2 and 3 until the cushion has an opaque, even finish. Most upholstery will need three layers of paint to achieve full coverage. Once the last layer of paint has fully dried, gently remove the painter's tape to reveal your restored seat cushions.

SAND IT SMOOTH *Don't be afraid to lightly sand painted vinyl or painted upholstery fabric between coats. This helps ensure that the next coat goes on evenly and blends smoothly with the first coat. The thicker the fabric, the more sanding will be needed. Chalk-based paints also work well on most linen and cotton fabrics. I don't recommend painting fabrics with a loose weave or high nap like velvet or tapestry because they will hold too much paint to achieve a smooth surface.*

PAINTING THE WOOD

Move the chairs to a well-ventilated but breeze-free area outside for this next phase to avoid inhaling harmful fumes. I recommend using a cardboard spray booth to protect the surface (see Create Your Own Spray Booth, page 26). Spray lacquers will dry very quickly in dry environments. However, humidity will lengthen the drying time.

5. Tape kraft paper over the painted seat cushions.

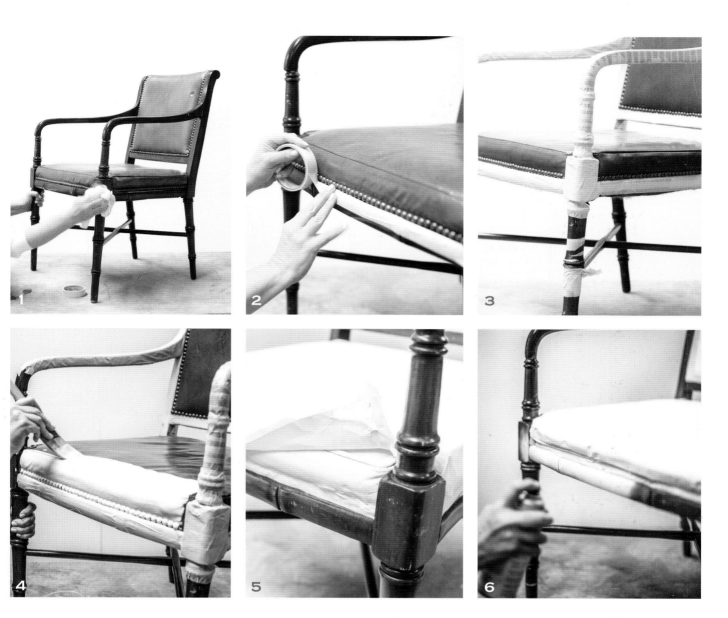

6. Holding the aerosol can about 10 inches (25 cm) from the wooden frame of the chairs, spray the lacquer on one section of the chair in long, even strokes. To avoid undesirable drips or gaps, rotate the chair to the next section you want to spray. Repeat until you have sprayed all sections of the frame. Most surfaces need two coats of lacquer to achieve an opaque finish. Let each coat dry completely (about 45 minutes to 1 hour) and sand it before applying the next coat. Once the final coat is dry, gently remove the kraft paper from the cushions. (You do not need to sand the final coat.)

7. Using a little clear wax on a clean rag, apply it to the vinyl cushions. Let it dry (about 20 minutes), then buff to the desired sheen.

THE LUCY COCKTAIL TABLE

Antiques aren't the only kind of furniture worth rescuing. You can also transform everyday items from a big-box store or a catalog. It's so much fun to turn a bore into a beauty! I bought this particular piece because I needed an end table. Now it blends well with my kitchen, and the top makes a stylish statement. The inspiration for this project is *églomisé*, a traditional French technique that involves etching on the back of glass. It sounds and looks fancy (and specialists charge a fortune to do it), but you'll be amazed to discover you can create a convincing alternative thanks to some simple droplets of water. *Églomisé* is also lovely for wall tiles or panels (adding sparkle in a dining room, for example) and for insets on furniture.

It's best to use a large adhesive mylar stencil for this project, ideally one that is a similar size to your tabletop or to the size of the stencil design you want on it. This way you won't have to move the stencil around, which makes it tricky to try to match up the edges, and you'll be able to create an even finish at one time, instead of in several rounds of spraying and drying. I recommend mylar because it is thicker and stays in place; if your stencil is not adhesive, you can use tape to hold it in place.

MATERIALS

2 cans of white spray lacquer

1 can of gold spray lacquer

Spray bottle

Kraft paper or paper towels

Adhesive mylar stencil in the pattern of your choice, preferably similar in size to your tabletop

2 clean, lint-free rags

Gentle degreaser

GETTING STARTED

PREPPING THE SURFACE
Some mass-produced furniture has a coating on it that can create a fish-eye effect when you try to apply a finish. It's important to clean this away so that your lacquer will look smooth and shiny. You'll also want to remove any surfactants from the tabletop so that you have a clean slate. Before you begin, remove the glass tabletop. Using a clean rag and a little degreaser, thoroughly scrub the top and set it aside on a level work surface. With a second clean rag, do the same for the table base.

PAINTING THE BASE
Be sure to lacquer the table in a well-ventilated but breeze-free area. A cardboard spray booth or box (see Create Your Own Spray Booth, page 26) is ideal. While glass like the top should not be sanded between coats of lacquer, and there is no need to sand metal, you will want to sand between coats if the base is made of wood.

1. Holding the spray can 10 inches (25 cm) from the base of the table, spray all the surfaces with white lacquer in long, even strokes. Let it dry completely (about 45 minutes to 1 hour). Sand the first layer of lacquer if the base is wood.

2. Repeat with another coat or two of white lacquer, sanding in between coats if the base is wood, to achieve full coverage. (You do not need to sand the final coat.)

CREATING THE *ÉGLOMISÉ* EFFECT
Instead of etching the glass in the typical way, this technique creates a beautifully imperfect look on the surface using the negative space from the water droplets. It's important to spray the water up into the air and let it fall naturally, rather than to spray it directly onto the surface. The idea behind *églomisé* is that you are working on the back of the glass. After your pattern is complete and dry, you will turn the glass over so that the gold-and-white *églomisé* decoration is visible through the clear top.

3. Fill the spray bottle with tap water. Set it to medium spray so that it will spray droplets, not a fine mist. Spray the water up in the air above the glass, allowing the water droplets to fall back down onto its surface. Move the bottle around as you spray to create a random, organic effect.

4. Holding the aerosol can 7 to 8 inches (18 to 20 cm) from the base of the table, spray the white lacquer on the wet surface in long, even strokes, being careful to overlap the edges. To avoid undesirable drips, do not linger in one area too long. Let the lacquer dry slightly for 2 to 3 minutes.

5, 6, and 7. Lightly cover the wet glass with kraft paper or paper towels. Press gently so that the water gets absorbed. (Try not to move the paper or towels side to side so the lacquer stays put.) Once all of the water is absorbed, gently lift up the paper or towels.

8. Let the surface dry completely (you can use a blow-dryer if you wish). You will see clear glass spots where the water droplets kept the lacquer from adhering.

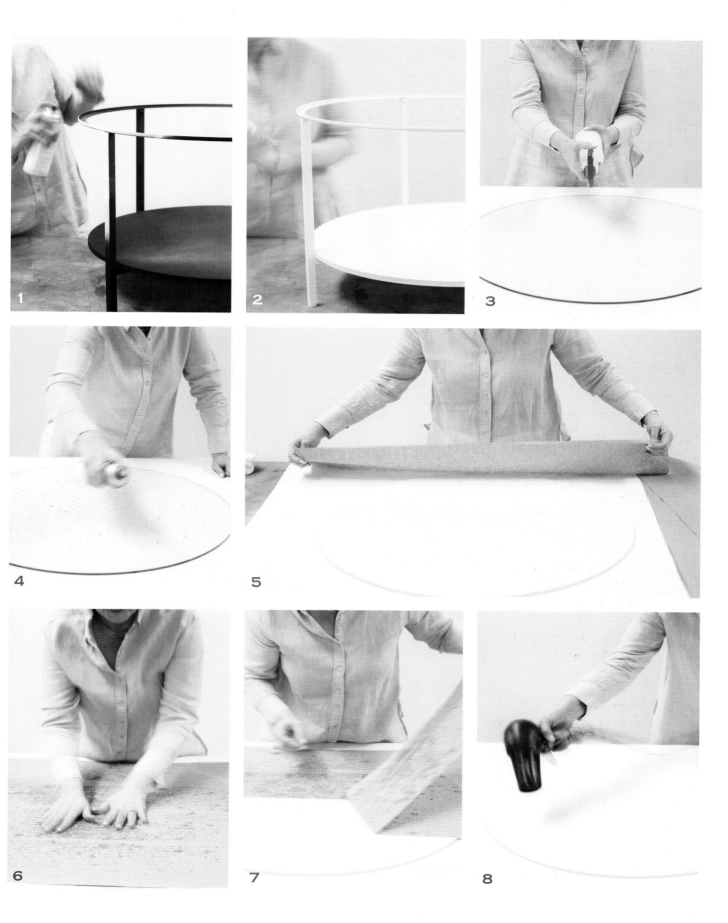

9. Lay the stencil down carefully on top of the glass. Holding the aerosol can 10 inches (25 cm) from the base of the table, spray the gold lacquer in long, even strokes, being careful to overlap the edges.

10. Carefully remove the stencil. Let the glass dry completely.

11 and 12. Holding the aerosol can 10 inches (25 cm) from the base of the table, spray the white lacquer over the entire tabletop. Let it dry completely. Repeat with a second coat of white lacquer. Once the glass top is completely dry, turn it over so that the pattern is on the underside, visible through the clear top, and place it back on the base.

CHAPTER 7

MILK PAINT (CASEIN PAINT)

Worn and aged finishes have the most magnificent imperfections. If you look closely at an antique, you will most likely see a spectrum of colors peeking through the finish, created by layers of paint. These charming cracks and peelings reveal a myriad of historical color trends. How enchanting to see life stories sandwiched on top of one another! In fact, I would bet that milk paint is one of the layers you see, as it is one of the oldest and most frequently used paint products in recorded history. The good news is this: Replicating antique finishes with milk paint is easy; it's practically the same material as it was a thousand years ago!

I also love how mixing up milk paint involves some incredibly easy DIY—another opportunity for creativity, which by now you know I can't resist. Milk paint is sold in a powder form, and all you need to do is combine it with water (for mixing tips, see Chapter 3, page 24). That means you can make your own color, blending a bit of this powder and a bit of that—as you'll see in the Amelia chairs project in this chapter. Whether I am after a chippy layered texture or a smooth striped contrast, milk paint is my go-to product for classically antiqued finishes.

This beautiful eighteenth-century reproduction uses a centuries-old formula of milk paint with gold-leaf accents.

Milk paint is thought to date back 8,000 to 20,000 years. Cave painters used a very crude form of milk paint. Over time, the formula changed for more durable results.

This highly carved
console was dressed
in milk paint. More
than one color was
used to create depth.

THE ELEONORA CONSOLE

MATERIALS

1 quart (960 ml) of gray chalk-based paint (optional)

1 cup (240 ml) of medium gray milk paint powder

1 cup (240 ml) of dark gray milk paint powder

1 bottle of antiquing glaze (about 2 cups [480 ml] needed)

1 tablespoon (15 ml) of light gray milk paint powder

1 tablespoon (15 ml) of black milk paint powder

1 bottle of natural liquid beeswax

Gilding size

Four 2-inch (5-cm) flat natural-bristle brushes

Round artist's brush (#12)

Cheesecloth

1 or 2 natural sea wool sponges

1 pad of #0000 steel wool

Small square of cardboard

Trowel

400 grit sandpaper

2 clean, lint-free rags

Gentle degreaser

3 small washable containers

Small disposable container

O ne of the great surprises of shopping in antiques flea markets is that you sometimes discover various parts of the same piece of furniture, separated from each other—and just waiting to be reunited! I might spot a single drawer here or there, or, as on one recent shopping trip, a marble top. Though I wasn't in the market for a console, I soon realized the ornately carved base I spotted in a booth across the way was meant to be married to my newly procured marble piece. At less than the price of a fancy dinner for two, this perfect duo was just too good to pass up. With some paint and antiquing on the base, the piece complemented the marble even more beautifully. In this project, you'll learn how to make a custom-colored wax, which you can use to bring depth and subtle richness to all kinds of furnishings and objects. If you apply a base coat of chalk-based paint first, as in this project, milk paint or a pigmented wax containing milk paint can then be used on all kinds of surfaces besides wood, like resin and plastic.

GETTING STARTED

PREPPING THE SURFACE
Because dust easily settles into all furniture crevices, a thorough cleaning is crucial to preparation.

1. Using a clean rag and a little degreaser, thoroughly scrub the console base.

PAINTING THE BASE
Milk paint does not contain any chemical adherents, so if you are working with a finished surface (for example, one that has shellac, lacquer, paint, or other industrial finishes), you'll need to apply a layer of chalk-based paint first as a base. See Chapter 3, page 24 for more on premixing milk paints the night before, which I recommend for the best result.

2. Dip a clean flat brush directly into the chalk-based paint if using it. Remove any excess paint by running the side of your brush across the inner lip of the container. Paint the console base using light, even strokes, and being careful to overlap the edges of each stroke. Let the paint dry completely (about 20 to 30 minutes).

3. In a small container, mix the medium gray milk paint powder and the dark gray milk paint powder together. Mix the combined powder with water in a 1 to 1 ratio (2 cups [480 ml] of warm tap water for every 2 cups [480 ml] of milk paint powder). Place a piece of cheesecloth over another small container and strain the milk paint solution to remove any lingering lumps and clumps.

4 and 5. Dip a flat brush directly into the milk paint. Paint the console base using light, even strokes and being careful to overlap the edges of each stroke. Let the paint dry completely (about 20 to 30 minutes). Repeat with a second layer of milk paint if needed to ensure an even, opaque finish on your base. Milk paint separates fairly quickly; stir it after each coat or dip of your brush as needed during application.

GLAZING THE BASE
Through all of my years dedicated to replicating fine antique finishes, I have found that antiquing glaze offers the most reliable and authentic results on wood and many different finishes. The glaze replicates the way the paint of a vintage piece of furniture would have pulled away, peeled, and cracked over time (in ways that sanding the paint down, another common antiquing method, cannot).

6. In the disposable container, dilute the antiquing glaze in a ratio of 2 parts warm tap water to 3 parts antiquing glaze (for example, 8 ounces [240 ml] of water for 12 ounces [360 ml] of glaze).

7 and 8. Dip a clean flat brush directly into the diluted glaze and remove any excess. Flick the solution over the entire milk-painted surface using your finger as shown.

9. Prepare a separate container of warm tap water. Dip a clean sponge into the diluted glaze, squeeze out the excess, and gently pat the raised and peripheral areas of the base

that would have received the most wear over time. Make only one pass with the sponge before cleaning it in the water. Continue to press and pat the sponge over these outer areas until you see the milk paint beginning to pull and crack away from the chalk-based paint layer beneath. Repeat the sponging process and cleaning process as needed until the desired amount of antiquing is achieved.

KEEP IT EVEN *Cleaning your sponge between each coat of antiquing glaze will help you avoid clumps and uneven application.*

GILDING THE BASE

Lightly gilded flecks complement ornately carved surfaces flawlessly. When adding gold leaf to a milk paint finish, you'll want to dim the shine so that only a few glimmers are left. Keep in mind: Most authentic, previously fully gilded antiquities have only 10 to 15 percent of their gilded layer left anyway.

10. Dip the tip of the artist's brush into the gilding size and remove any excess. Gently roll the side of the brush over the outermost portions of some of the carvings. After about 15 minutes, the size solution will turn from milky-white to clear. Test the size to see if it has come to tack by touching it with the tip of your ring finger; you're looking for a gentle pull.

11 and 12. Once this tack is evident, apply a full sheet of gold leaf to one of the areas you would like to gild: Holding the gold-leaf booklet taut at the folded portion of tissue paper near the spine on one side and at the other edge as shown, place the gold leaf against the surface and slowly pull away the single folded tissue sheet near the spine. (If you're gilding rounded hardware, wrap an entire sheet of gold leaf around the perimeter of the handles, as shown on page 61.) Burnish the tissue paper side of the booklet by pressing hard with your fingertips in one direction to adhere the gold-leaf sheet below to the size, and pull the booklet away.

13 and 14. Gently swipe away any loose shards of gold leaf with a clean flat brush. Let the size dry completely (about 1 hour after you applied it). Repeat steps 10 through 13 until all desired portions are dressed in an authentic gilded residue.

15. To finish the antiqued gilding process, dim the shiny gold leaf by brushing the gilded accents gently with the steel wool.

Milk paint and gold leaf—aged as if worn away over time— harmonize beautifully on the console.

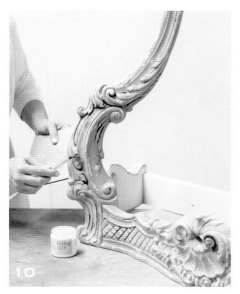

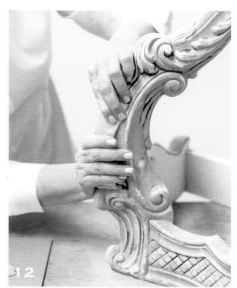

WAXING THE BASE

All-natural mediums can often be combined to create brand-new colorants and agents. Liquid beeswax and milk paint powder are the perfect examples. Here you'll mix the two to create a new version of colored wax.

16. Squeeze 2 tablespoons (30 ml) of liquid beeswax onto a square of cardboard, then add 1 tablespoon (15 ml) of the light gray milk paint powder and 1 tablespoon (15 ml) of black milk paint powder directly into the wax.

17. Using the trowel, blend the pigments and wax together until a smooth, colored wax forms.

18. Dip the tip of a clean flat brush into the pigmented wax and remove any excess. Using very light brush strokes, paint the outer areas of the legs and trim of the base to create subtle accents.

Let the wax dry for about 20 minutes. Using a clean rag, buff the waxed surface to enhance the depth and shine.

BUFFING THE MARBLE TOP

The stone elements on genuine antiquities do not typically possess a high shine. Not only would age have dulled the surface, but the finishing tools of the distant past would most likely not have produced a smooth polish. When you want to replicate the look of aged stone, you can turn a gloss finish into an authentic-looking matte finish with this wet sanding technique.

19. Dip the sandpaper into a container of water and gently buff the marble along the lines of its grain until a matte finish is achieved. Be careful to keep the surface wet during the entire sanding process.

Two consoles, two moods: one in a single color of milk paint alone (aged with an antiquing glaze), one with a second color as an accent and gold leaf as a third color and embellishment.

THE AMELIA CHAIRS

MATERIALS

½ cup (120 ml) of gray milk paint powder

1½ cups (360 ml) of blue milk paint powder

1 bottle of antiquing glaze

1 container of light antique wax

1 container of dark antique wax

3 or more 2-inch (5-cm) flat natural-bristle brushes

2 or more natural sea wool sponges

2 small squares of cardboard

Painter's tape (optional)

2 clean, lint-free rags

Gentle degreaser

2 small glass or plastic containers

Spoons for mixing (preferably plastic)

CREATING A CUSTOM COLOR *One of my favorite things about milk paints is that you can make endless custom colors. It's important to use milk paint made with natural pigments only, not synthetic, for a quality result. Natural milk paints come in a powder form that is true in color to the result you can expect, so the best way to see how your custom color will turn out is to mix the powdered paints together before adding water.*

Once you have a color you love, make a note of how you made it so that you don't forget! I bought a blank Moleskine journal for recording my custom colors. To make your own record, mix up the paint (always in a ratio of 1 part powder to 1 part warm tap water). Once you have the desired color in powder form, dip your finger in the paint, make a dot in the journal, and label it with the amounts of each milk paint color you used.

Caned chairs are such an overlooked find! Because it is so expensive to have a chair recaned, you can often find a perfectly elegant pair with tons of potential that the owners or antiques dealers have just chucked because one or both of the seats have holes. Keep an eye out for these in your curbside shopping! With some antiquing and a new seat cover to complement the original caned backs, this project will land you with some adorable extra chairs. The bluish-gray color and the sweet seat covers give them a very French flair. Be sure to premix your milk paint powders with water the night before for a smooth, easy-to-apply consistency (see Chapter 3, page 24).

GETTING STARTED

PREPPING THE SURFACE

While I painted the chairs freehand, you could tape around the frame so that you don't risk getting paint on the caning.

1. Using a clean rag and a gentle degreaser, thoroughly scrub the frame and caning. If desired, tape around the frame.

ANTIQUING THE FRAME

Some rules are made to be broken. Typically, we would use a coat of chalk-based paint on rescued furniture that already has a finish on it before using milk paint, so that the less-adherent milk paint has something to stick to. This project calls for painting directly on top of the piece, because we're going to antique it next and it's OK if some of the milk paint comes off and the stained finish peeks through; this just adds to the sense of age and depth. Also, you can expect less wear on the frame of a chair than on a dresser or tabletop, so you don't have to be as concerned about scratches from keys and purses and such. The chairs are distressed pretty heavily here as the desired effect is more provincial, less perfect.

2. Premix custom milk paint (see page 24). While we use just one layer of milk paint here, up to three milk paint colors can be layered in conjunction with an antiquing glaze to mimic a century-long cycle of polishing and painting. I recommend applying a full, opaque layer of each paint for optimal results, which may require two or three coats of each. I usually apply all three layers of paint, letting them dry completely in between, and then I will antique them at the end. You could also try antiquing the layers as you go.

CUSTOM CUSHIONS *I bought an 8-inch- (20-cm-) thick piece of foam and sewed a cushion cover with a skirt for it. If sewing is not one of your skills, there are plenty of charming ready-made options available at home stores, and lots of upholsterers who would be willing to indulge your custom project.*

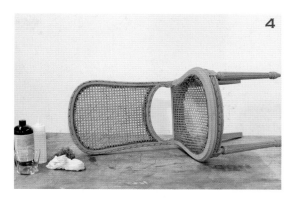

3. Dip a clean brush into your premixed custom milk paint solution. Paint the frame of the chairs. Let them dry completely (about 20 to 30 minutes). Prepare a container of warm tap water. In a separate container, saturate the sponge in the antiquing glaze. Squeeze out any excess. Sponge the glaze over the areas that would be most likely to get wear, such as the chair legs. Make only one pass with the sponge before cleaning it in the water. Once it's clean, repeat the sponging process and cleaning process as needed until the desired amount of antiquing is achieved.

CAN YOU GO TOO FAR? *It's important to clean the sponge between each pass with the antiquing glaze. Because the glaze lifts away paint, the sponge can get gunked up, and you don't want to be adding paint back onto the frame. Not sure how far to go with the antiquing? I recommend stopping a little before you think you're done. You won't know until the piece is dried and waxed how much paint you've removed, and I am often surprised at how much I've lifted up along the way. If I find I have taken off too much, I will sometimes tape my index finger with painter's tape, dip it into the milk paint (be sure to stir again with a spoon before you do, since it will likely have separated while you were antiquing the frame), and touch up the surface with dabs of paint where I feel I have taken off too much.*

WAXING THE FRAME

This combination of light wax with hints of dark wax is a go-to for protecting your finish, and it adds another layer of depth to the antiqued effect.

4. Dip a clean brush into the light antique wax and remove any excess on a clean piece of cardboard. Brush the wax over the entire frame. Let it dry for 10 to 15 minutes, then test the wax to see if it has come to tack by touching it with the tip of your ring finger; you're looking for a gentle pull.

5. After the light antique wax has come to tack, dip a clean brush into the dark antique wax and remove any excess. Brush the dark wax over the areas you want to age a little more, like the legs. Let the dark wax dry and come to tack (about 30 minutes). Using a clean rag, buff the newly waxed areas to the desired sheen.

6. Add the cushions.

BELLA WALL ART

MATERIALS

Venetian plaster powder (about 1 cup [240 ml] needed)

Burlap, cut to your desired size

2 or 3 colors of natural (not synthetic) milk paint powder (I used ochre and salmon colors, about ½ cup [120 ml] each)

1 booklet of gold leaf

Water-based gilding size

Three or four 2-inch (5-cm) flat natural-bristle brushes

Round artist's brush (#12)

Blender (see For Paint Only, page 18) or metal whisk

Metal putty knife

Spray bottle

Metal plaster trowel

Cheesecloth

3 small squares of cardboard

Squeezable bottle (such as a plastic water bottle)

1 pad of #0000 steel wool

Plastic or glass containers (such as a Mason jar with the lid)

This project will add magic to any home, no matter how small or large. It was inspired by the kind of gorgeous, crumbling plaster you might find in ancient Italian ruins, from Pompeii to Venice and beyond. The idea is so simple—you're dressing up (and aging) a basic fabric. You might choose to frame the result as if it were a piece of antique art (I dry-mounted mine on a piece of linen board and hung it in an acrylic frame), or you might even fall in love with this technique and decide to create enough pieces to use side by side as wallpaper. The aging process here involves a certain degree of precision, but with the experience under your belt by now, I think you'll find the result well worth your efforts.

1

2

GETTING STARTED

"PLASTERING" THE BURLAP
Plaster powder transforms simple burlap into a thick, continuous canvas for aging effects—and for your imagination to run wild.

1 and 2. Spread the burlap out flat on the work surface. In a small glass container, mix 1 part Venetian plaster with 1 part warm tap water. A blender works well to remove the lumps so that the mixture will be smooth; a metal whisk is another option. You're aiming for the consistency of very thick sour cream. Feel free to add a little more warm water to make it smoother.

3 and 4. With a metal putty knife (do not use plastic), apply the Venetian plaster over the entire surface of the burlap, filling in any holes in the material. Let it dry completely; this could take 1 to 2 hours or longer.

PAINTING AND AGING THE PLASTER

With a few different colors of milk paint, you can embellish your surface in an ombré fashion that suggests walls darkening or fading through centuries of age. You can either begin with the lightest paint at the bottom of your plastered burlap "canvas" and use darker paints as you go up, or begin with the darkest paint at the bottom (as shown). The trowel will remove some of the plaster and cause the paint colors to overlap, creating a beautiful finish right before your eyes. Don't worry about making it look perfect. There is no real science to it, and the intention is that no two pieces will be the same (also, as with anything artistic, you'll gain more expertise with this technique as you practice). See Chapter 3, page 24 for more on premixing milk paints for an optimal result. Milk paint solution separates quickly, so you'll need to stir the paint occasionally during application.

5. Using a spray bottle filled with warm tap water, gently mist the dried canvas to soften it.

6. In a small container, mix 1 part warm tap water with 1 part milk paint (½ cup [120 ml] of each). Place a piece of cheesecloth over another small container and strain the milk paint solution to remove any lingering lumps and clumps. Repeat to mix each color you are using.

7. Using a 2-inch (5-cm) flat bristle brush, splatter your chosen color of milk paint onto the canvas in a horizontal direction, starting from the bottom and going up about one-third of the height of your plastered burlap. Reload your brush with milk paint and brush it on horizontally using a very light stroke; the effect should be similar to a watercolor wash. The thin paint will be absorbed into the surface very quickly.

8. Using a clean flat bristle brush, repeat step 7 with your next color or colors of milk paint on the next third of the canvas.

9. After applying all of your colors, while the paint is still wet, drag the metal trowel from the top of the canvas to the bottom, blending the paint colors as you go and removing any excess on a square of cardboard as it builds up on the trowel. New colors will emerge as the blended paint starts to overlap.

BLEND CAREFULLY *Don't overdo the blending or you will start to lose the depth in your finish and it will get messy. Stop as soon as you are happy with the way it looks.*

---

10. Using the squeeze bottle filled with warm tap water and holding your canvas upright, squeeze water over the semi-wet canvas to allow the paint to blend and to look as though water has dripped on the wall fragment over many years. It's best to work from left to right, squeezing the drips out at a smooth, quick pace and holding the bottle at a 45-degree angle. Be careful not to overdo the dripping; you don't want to saturate the surface. Let the paint dry completely (about 20 to 30 minutes).

11

12

13

GILDING THE PLASTER

Gilding is optional, but it adds another layer of depth and age to the plaster. Instead of an all-over effect as we often use on hardware, here you will gild only the bottom third of your plaster. As opposed to the usual gilding technique, which requires full coverage with size before you apply the leaf, you will use less size so that the leaf adheres imperfectly to the plaster and pulls away irregularly.

11. Dip the tip of the artist's brush into the gilding size. Remove any excess size on a clean square of cardboard. There shouldn't be much size left on the brush as you want to dry-brush it onto the plaster. Apply size only to the bottom quarter of the plaster. You do not want full coverage here; "holidays" (gaps) in the size are desirable so the gold leaf only sticks to the size in random patches. After about 15 minutes, the size solution will turn from milky-white to clear. (It may come to tack a little more quickly since the plaster is absorbent.) Test the size to see if it has come to tack by touching it with the tip of your ring finger; you're looking for a gentle pull.

12. Once this tack is evident, apply a full sheet of gold leaf: Holding the gold-leaf booklet taut at the folded portion of tissue paper near the spine on one side and at the other edge as shown, place the gold leaf against the surface and slowly pull away the single folded tissue sheet near the spine. Burnish the tissue paper side of the booklet by pressing with your fingertips in one direction to adhere the gold-leaf sheet below to the size, and pull the booklet away. Repeat in the next area of plaster, overlapping with the edge of the previous leaf, until you have covered the bottom quarter of the canvas where you applied the size.

13. Using a clean 2-inch (5-cm) flat bristle brush, remove the excess gold leaf that isn't sticking to the size.

14. Using the steel wool, gently rub off more of the excess leaf. Be careful not to rub too hard; if you do, the graphite gray steel wool color will get on your plaster. Let it dry completely (about 30 minutes).

14

15

16

CRACKING THE PLASTER

This rolling technique will cause the plaster to crack randomly and naturally, which is just what we're looking for. You can repeat this step to your liking; I usually do it just once or twice on each side of the canvas so that the cracks don't get too small.

15. Starting at the bottom of the canvas, roll up the piece so that you have one circular loop as shown. Press down on the roll. The plaster will start to chip and fall off. Roll the canvas over on itself again. Press down. Repeat until the whole canvas is rolled up, pressing down each time you make a full loop.

16. Unroll the canvas. Flip it over and repeat step 14 on the other side.

17. Repeat steps 14 and 15 as desired.

CREATING WALLPAPER *Available at fabric stores or online, burlap comes in large rolls, usually 36 to 46 inches (91 to 116 cm) wide and often in 10- or 20-yard (9- or 18-m) rolls. If you're creating an individual piece of wall art as I did here, you can buy a piece of burlap cut to size before you begin. If you plan to use the finished plastered burlap as wallpaper, you may need two to three large rolls, depending on the yardage and the size of your room. I recommend doing this in a room with a maximum wall height of 10 feet (3 m). You will create the Bella Wall Art treatment on one long single roll that will stretch from floor to ceiling; be sure to leave 3 to 5 inches (7.5 to 13 cm) of extra material at both ends to allow for the ceiling and base molding trims. I suggest skipping the gilding step for wallpaper, since it becomes difficult to line up the gilding convincingly on the many sections of wallpaper you'll need to overlap at the edges to cover a whole wall.*

CHAPTER 8
ANTIQUED MIRRORS

It may never have occurred to you that those heavenly aged mirrors you see in French bistros are at your fingertips—literally. You can have that perfectly imperfect look, that dreamy constellation of darker and lighter silver spots, and you don't have to wait decades for time to give it to you.

The secret is the back of the mirror. If you strip away the opaque backing of a real mirror, you can then use an antiquing solution to age and etch the silver beneath, and the effects will show through the glass front. Or you can use water (yes, water!) and lacquer on glass to create an aged effect that resembles the gilded beauty of *verre églomisé*, a highly sought-after French technique of etching or back-painting and gilding glass that can cost many thousands of dollars. We'll use both of these techniques in the projects to follow. I encourage you to think beyond the traditional rectangular mirrors you'd hang up or pose on a mantelpiece (though, of course, don't hesitate to try this technique for those!). Imagine the other exciting possibilities, such as adding mirrored accents on dressers and headboards, creating mirrored tabletops, even (one day, perhaps!) covering your wall with mirrored tiles.

After all, why not shoot for the stars once you have built your repertoire of finishes? Of all the spaces I've ever seen, the Hall of Mirrors at Versailles remains one of the most inspiring. Fortunately for all of us non-royals, we can bring an undeniable sense of luxury and sophistication into our homes with antiqued mirrors, reflecting our sense of taste as well as the beautiful and meaningful treasures that adorn our rooms.

Have you ever wondered why some antique mirrors are sectioned into two pieces? In the sixteenth and seventeenth centuries, the process limited the size. Taxation also played a role; the larger the single piece of mirror, the higher the tax.

Thinking beyond the mirror as mirror can inspire you to antique mirrors on tabletops, as accents on sideboards, chests, armoires, and more. The classic framed mantel mirror is a good place to start.

THE SELZNICK CABINET

A cabinet of this size can become the visual anchor of your whole room. Why not have fun with it, dress it up, and make it truly special? The original piece was a little humdrum, but it offered a great canvas for bright color, a simple switch to the hardware, and some antiqued mirror that takes it to another level. One of the benefits of creating fabulous and affordable pieces yourself is that it leaves more room in your budget for buying gorgeous art and—a great love of mine and maybe yours—flowers and plants that bring your room to vibrant life.

MATERIALS

1 quart (960 ml) of bright blue-green chalk-based paint

1 quart (960 ml) of black chalk-based paint

1 can of dark blue spray lacquer

1 can of clear high-gloss spray lacquer

1 bottle of mirror stripping solution

1 bottle of mirror antiquing solution

1 container of mirror mastic

1 container of silicone

Raw wood drawer pulls

Real mirror panels, cut to size

Two 2-inch (5-cm) flat synthetic-bristle brushes

Two 2-inch (5-cm) flat foam brushes

Screwdriver

Caulking gun

400 grit sandpaper

Spray bottle with a fine mist setting

Kraft paper

Masking tape

Paper mask

Protective gloves

Protective eyewear

4 clean, lint-free rags

Gentle, non-oily degreaser

Large plastic container or tub

GETTING STARTED

PREPPING THE SURFACE

This particular piece was rescued from a trash heap, so it was especially important to remove the grease and other surfactants on the wood to allow the chalk-based paint to go on flawlessly. If you're keeping the hardware on your piece, you can tape around it to protect it from the paint. If you're replacing the hardware, it's easiest if you remove it before you start painting. I didn't do that here because I thought I would keep it until inspiration struck, so I removed the hardware when the painting was already in process.

1. Remove the metal hardware with a screwdriver. Using a clean rag and a little degreaser, thoroughly scrub the entire dresser.

PAINTING THE DRESSER

A lacquer would have been beautiful for the whole piece, but the color I envisioned for the dresser didn't exist in a spray lacquer, so I had a little fun coming up with a substitute! A similar but less time-consuming glossy finish is achieved thanks to a top coat of clear high-gloss lacquer over the bright blue-green chalk-based paint. As always, when working with lacquer, it's important to avoid inhaling harmful fumes by working in a well-ventilated but breeze-free area. See Create Your Own Spray Booth, page 26, for how to create a simple shadowbox.

2. Dip the tip of a bristle brush directly into the can of bright blue-green chalk-based paint. Remove any excess paint by running the side of your brush across the inner lip of the can. Apply the paint using long, even strokes, and being careful to overlap the edges of each stroke. Let it dry completely (about 20 to 30 minutes). Repeat with a second coat to achieve an opaque finish. Let it dry completely.

3. Holding the can of clear high-gloss lacquer 10 inches (25 cm) from the surface of the cabinet, spray it evenly. Let it dry completely (at least 1 hour).

LACQUERING THE HARDWARE

It's easy to find raw wood hardware like these pulls, and lacquering these smaller elements adds another high-gloss accent with much less work. Before you begin, lightly sand the wood pulls to ensure a smooth surface for the lacquer.

4. Spray the pulls evenly with the dark blue lacquer. Let them dry completely (about 45 minutes to 1 hour). Lightly sand the lacquered surface and dust well with a clean rag to remove any residue from sanding. Repeat step 4 with a second coat of lacquer to achieve an opaque finish. Let the pulls dry completely, then spray them evenly with the high-gloss sealer. Let them dry completely.

5

STRIPPING AND ANTIQUING THE MIRROR

Stripping the backing off your mirror ensures that you'll see the aging effects clearly from the front. See page 130 for instructions on how to measure the dimensions of your mirror panels so that you can have them pre-cut for you. I like to work on all of the mirror panels at once, first stripping all of them and then antiquing all of them. Because the antiquing solution works best on a wet mirror, you'll want to proceed directly to that step after stripping the back of the mirror. It's important to take precautions with the mirror stripping solution; follow the manufacturer's instructions and be sure to do this step in a well-ventilated area wearing a paper mask and protective gloves that cover your wrists.

5. Using a foam brush and wearing protective gloves and eyewear, spread a uniform amount of stripping solution over the nonshiny back side of the mirror panels. Do not use too much, as this can prevent the solution from activating.

6. Leave the solution to activate for 5 to 10 minutes—5 is average. It will cause the backing paint to start bubbling up and "moving." Meanwhile, prepare the spray bottle with a solution of 1 part non-oily degreaser with 1 part water.

7. While the solution is bubbling, cut out sheets of kraft paper that are slightly larger than each mirror panel. Once all of the backing looks like it has bubbled up, place the sheet of kraft paper on top of the loosened backing paint. Lightly smooth out the kraft paper and press down so that the backing paint adheres to it.

8. Gently lift the edge of the kraft paper and remove it from each mirror panel. Most, if not all, of the backing paint will lift off with the kraft paper. You will likely see some leftover copper coloring—a reddish-orange color.

9. Using a clean foam brush, apply another light coat of stripping solution on the exposed silver backing of the mirror panels and gently agitate the solution with your brush until all of the copper color is removed and the mirror backing is a clear-white or silver color. You may need to press down a little harder with the foam brush to remove the last bits of residue.

10. Fill a large container half-full of water. Holding each mirror at an angle, spray on the diluted degreaser and remove the excess

stripping solution on the back with a clean rag, bathing it with the water from the bath. Be very careful not to scratch the exposed silver while cleaning the back.

11. Place the wet mirrors on a flat surface with the backing side facing up again. Saturate a clean rag with the mirror antiquing solution and lightly sponge it over the entire exposed silver backing side of each mirror using a patting motion. Let it activate for 15 to 20 minutes. The surface should begin to tarnish and turn a rainbow of colors as it ages and oxidizes the silver of the mirror.

12. Check the front of the mirror to see if the tarnishing of the back side is to your taste. If not, continue to apply a little more of the antique mirror solution and allow it to activate until you've reached the desired appearance. (Not pictured.)

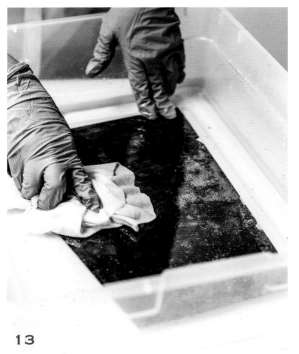

13

14

13. Using a clean rag and a clean water bath, bathe the back of each mirror to remove the antiquing solution and stop the etching process. Let the mirror air-dry (about 20 to 30 minutes), or use a small circular fan to expedite the drying process.

14. Once each mirror is dry, dip a clean bristle brush into the black chalk-based paint and remove any excess. Apply a coat of the black chalk-based paint to the silver backing to protect it. (You can also spray the coat of paint.) Let it dry completely (about 20 to 30 minutes). Repeat with another coat or until the back has an opaque, even coverage.

ATTACHING THE MIRROR PANELS

Mastic is often used to attach mirrors, but it takes quite a while to dry. My trick is to alternate dabs of mastic with dabs of silicone, which dries almost immediately. You can use this combination technique to attach all kinds of mirrors and mirrored details that will end up in a vertical position—on walls and headboards, for example. The masking tape helps ensure that your panels won't slide as they're drying.

15. Using a caulking gun, squeeze a dime-sized dollop of the mirror mastic onto the corner of the area of the drawer where you will be applying the mirror. Repeat around the perimeter of the inset, spacing each dollop out about 3 inches (7.5 cm). Using the caulking gun, squeeze a dime-sized dollop of the silicone in the space between every two dollops of mirror mastic.

16. Carefully adhere each mirror panel. Apply masking tape over the panels to hold them in place during drying. Let them dry completely (4 to 5 hours) before removing the tape.

17. Replace the hardware, then place the completed drawers back in the dresser.

15

16

So many pieces of furniture and cabinets have a recessed door or drawer panel. This is perfect for adding an antiqued mirror inset.

17

THE DRAKE LANTERN

While we were putting the finishing touches on our home's little loggia, I began to look around for outdoor-friendly lights that could add ambience, texture, and charm to our fresh-air escape. Of course, the Italian lantern I fell in love with also came with a price tag of thousands of dollars. Though similarly shaped vintage fixtures are pretty common, none would have the antique glass panels or Italian pitted silver frame that were irresistible to me. With some diligent research, I devised a plan that would give my flea market steal every bit of that luxurious designer finish. The key here is to use sterling-silver leaf, which takes on an amazing sense of age thanks to a magical solution, and to buy real mirror, which will respond to the stripping and antiquing solutions in a similarly remarkable way. This project is not for the faint of heart, but if you take it step by step, the results are well worth the wait.

MATERIALS

1 booklet of sterling-silver leaf

1 bottle of zinc antiquing solution

1 bottle of mirror stripping solution

1 bottle of mirror antiquing solution

1 pint (480 ml) of chalk-based paint in the color of your choice for the backing

Gilding size

2-inch (5-cm) flat synthetic-bristle brush

Slender, tapered artist's brush such as a round #12

3-inch (7.5-cm) flat foam brush

4 mirror panels, cut to size (see page 144)

Scissors

Natural seeded cotton batting

1 pad of #0000 steel wool

Spray bottle with a fine mist setting

Kraft paper

Permanent marker

1 container of silicone

Paper mask

Protective gloves

Gentle, non-oily degreaser

Clean, lint-free rags

Glass or plastic container

Large washable container

GETTING STARTED

PREPPING THE SURFACE

You may not realize that rust will continue to corrode metal even after it has been painted. It's important to clean, remove, or seal any rust you find before painting. You will need to have mirror panels cut to fit each panel before you begin. Most local hardware stores sell and trim real mirror pieces. Vintage iron isn't generally known for its precise composition, so to be safe, you'll want to make a template of each panel of your lantern by tracing the shape of each panel on a piece of kraft paper with a pen or marker, cutting the shapes out, and bringing them to the shop.

1. Using a clean rag and a little degreaser, thoroughly scrub the entire body of the metal lantern and the mirror panels.

APPLYING THE SILVER

Two of the most important rules of applying sterling-silver leaf are to never touch the unsealed silver leaf in the booklet and to always work in a breeze-free area. The oils on your fingers could leave an impression on the sensitive sterling silver, and the leaf is thin enough to blow away. Before you begin, cut the silver leaf booklet down to the size needed to cover each thin section of the frame so that you can conserve the rest of the booklet for other projects.

2. Holding the spine of the sterling-silver leaf booklet in one hand, trim the entire booklet down to a little larger than the width of the frame, leaving room for overlap on each side.

3. Dip the artist's brush into the gilding size. Remove any excess glue by running the side of your brush across the lip of the container. Apply a full-coverage layer of size to one side of the lantern frame's exterior. (There is no need to apply silver leaf to the interior as your glass will cover it.) After about 15 minutes, the size solution will turn from milky-white to clear. Test the size to see if it has come to tack by touching it with the tip of your ring finger; you're looking for a gentle pull.

4 and 5. Once this tack is evident, apply a trimmed-to-size sheet of silver leaf: Pull the protective tissue paper over the top sheet of silver leaf back toward the spine. Holding the booklet from the back so that you don't touch the silver leaf, lay the silver side of the booklet against the surface of the frame, wrapping it around the front, and slowly pull away the single folded tissue sheet near the spine. Burnish the tissue paper side of the booklet by pressing with your fingertips in one direction to adhere the silver leaf sheet below to the size, and pull the booklet away. Repeat steps 3 to 5, one side of the lantern at a time, until the entire lantern is covered in silver leaf. Let the size dry completely (about 1 hour after you applied it).

6. Brushing in one direction only, gently swipe the flat bristle brush over the surface of the frame to remove any loose shards of silver leaf.

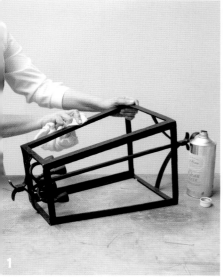

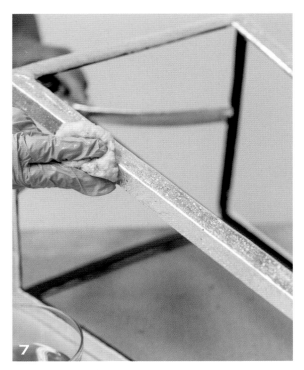

ANTIQUING THE SILVER

Zinc antiquing solution can also be used to oxidize and age silver. It's important to use a glass or plastic container for zinc solution, not a metal container since it could react, and always wear protective gloves.

7. In a glass or plastic container, dip a handful of cotton batting into the zinc antiquing solution. Squeeze out the excess and firmly pat down one entire side of the silver-leafed frame.

8. While the zinc solution is still beaded up and wet, fill a fine mist sprayer with 1 part mirror antiquing solution and 1 part warm tap water (¼ cup [60 ml] of each), then apply a fine layer over the zinc. After a few minutes, the shiny silver will begin to darken. Repeat steps 7 and 8 on each side until the entire silver-leafed frame is covered

in the zinc solution and misted with the antiquing solution. Let it dry completely (about 2 to 3 hours).

9. To uncover the oxidized layer of silver and accomplish the Italian pitted silver effect, lightly rub the silver leaf with the steel wool after it has dried overnight.

Gilding with a twist! Imitation gold, silver, or other metal leaf will not "age." Using sterling-silver leaf is a must to "antique" the silver and achieve something special.

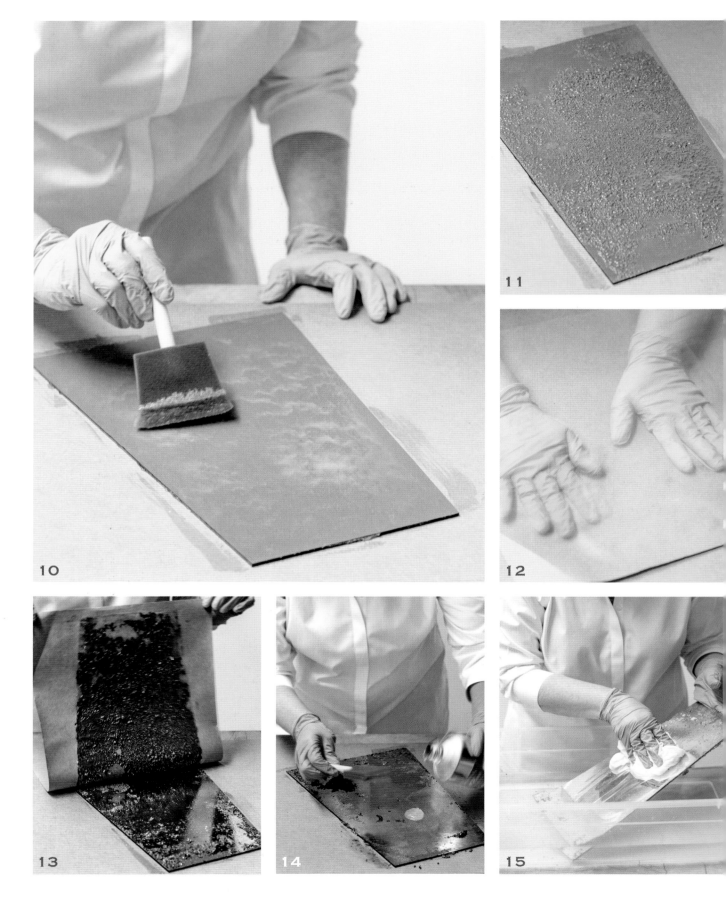

STRIPPING THE MIRROR

While this Old World European finish is delicate in appearance, the execution requires some elbow grease. These next steps must be done in a well-ventilated and well-lit area; the fumes and ingredients in mirror stripping solution should be used with caution. Be sure to wear a paper mask and protective gloves and follow the manufacturer's directions. Warmer weather helps activate the stripping solution more quickly.

FRONT OR BACK *Use a permanent marker to label the front (glass) side of each mirror panel. (Once you've stripped the mirror backing, you won't be able to tell one side from the other.)*

10. Using the foam brush, spread a uniform amount of stripping solution over the nonshiny back side of the mirror. Do not use too much as this can prevent the solution from activating.

11. Leave the solution to activate for 5 to 10 minutes—5 is average. It will cause the backing paint to start bubbling up and "moving." Meanwhile, prepare a spray bottle with a solution of 1 part non-oily degreaser to 1 part water.

12. While the solution is bubbling, cut out sheets of kraft paper that are slightly larger than each mirror panel. Once all of the backing looks like it has bubbled up, place the sheet of kraft paper on top of the loosened backing paint. Lightly smooth out the kraft paper and press down so that the backing paint adheres to it.

13. Gently lift the edge of the kraft paper and remove it from the mirror. Most, if not all, of the backing paint will lift off with the kraft paper. You will likely see some leftover copper coloring—a reddish-orange color.

14. Using a clean foam brush, apply another light coat of stripping solution on the exposed silver backing of the mirror and gently agitate the solution with the brush until all of the copper color is removed and the mirror backing is a clear-white or silver color. You may need to press down a little harder with the foam brush to remove the last bits of residue.

15. Fill the large washable container half-full with water. To clean the mirror, spray the entire back panel with the diluted degreaser to neutralize the stripping solution, holding the mirror at an angle over the prepared water bath. Submerge the panel in the water bath. Bathe the mirror with the water and a clean rag until all of the stripping solution and gray backing are removed, and pat the panels dry. Be very careful not to scratch the exposed silver while cleaning the back.

ANTIQUING THE MIRROR

Less is more when it comes to antiquing mirrors, but you can always reapply the mirror antiquing solution with a mister or a spray bottle after the first rinse. Using the mist setting for the second pass will result in a more even mottling, whereas using a typical spray bottle application will give the mirror a more clustered, random, and imperfect set of age spots comparable to the look of mercury glass—very desirable if you want an authentic aged look. In this case, I realized the caramel and brown tones of my glass panel could use a little more depth, so I used a mister bottle for a second pass. It's best to work on one panel at a time, no matter how confident you feel in your skill set. Continue to wear your protective gloves and paper mask and to work in a well-ventilated area for the antiquing process.

16. Prepare a water bath in a clean, washable container. Place the mirror on a flat surface with the backing side facing up again. Saturate a clean rag with the mirror antiquing solution and squeeze out the excess; using a patting motion, lightly sponge it over the entire exposed silver backing side. Aim for full coverage, but if you intentionally skip from one area to another as you pat, this will result in a more natural-looking sporadic effect than if you apply the solution in lines. Allow the solution to sit for 15 minutes. The surface should begin to tarnish and turn a rainbow of colors as it ages and oxidizes the silver of the mirror. Check the front of the mirror periodically to see if the tarnishing of the back side is to your taste.

REFLECT ON THIS *One way to monitor the reaction on the mirror's silver is to place a piece of white paper in front of the mirror when you lift it up. This will give you an ideal reflection.*

17. Once you're satisfied with the darkening of the mirror's reaction, using a clean rag, bathe the back of the mirror in the water bath to remove the antiquing solution and stop the etching process.

18 and 19. If desired, make a second application of the mirror antiquing solution with a spray bottle on the typical or fine mist setting. Be sure to check frequently during this second application to be sure the mirror isn't getting too dark for your taste. Once satisfied, bathe the mirror in the water bath to stop the antiquing process and remove any remaining solution. Let it dry completely (about 20 to 30 minutes) or use a small circular fan to expedite the drying process.

20. Once the mirror is dry, dip a clean bristle brush into the chalk-based paint color of your choice and remove any excess. (You can also spray paint, as I did here.) Apply an even coat to the silver backing to protect it. Let it dry completely (about 20 to 30 minutes). Repeat with another coat or two until the back has an opaque, even coverage.

CHOOSE YOUR COLOR *The paint color you select for the back will be visible from the front, so pick something you will love as part of the overall aesthetic picture.*

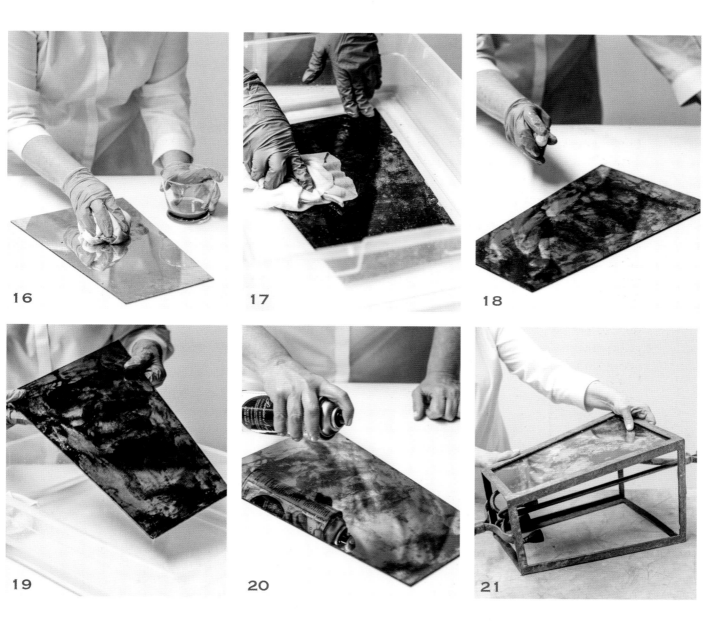

ASSEMBLING THE LANTERN

My lantern wasn't ever meant to have window panels, so instead of being able to rest the glass on a preexisting lip below them, I needed to adhere my antiqued panels to the lantern's surface with silicone.

21. Once the paint is dry on each mirror panel, attach one of them to the lantern's surface using silicone. Lay the lantern flat, with that panel facing up, to dry overnight. Repeat on the other three sides.

The French commode (left) features antiqued silver gilding and antiqued mirror inset into the doors and drawer. A "sunburst" mirror frame with antiqued silver gilt and an antiqued mirror helps connect a collection of gilded accessories below.

Silver meets gold in this ornate gilded frame for an antiqued mirror. A wall of sectioned antiqued mirror (opposite) has abundant impact.

THE ALFRED MIRROR TRAY

Mirrored trays add such a welcome, portable sparkle to any surface. They're wonderful for carrying icy lemonade—or something stronger—to guests, and they do double duty sprucing up the room, reflecting light and whatever lovely objects you place on top. This tray was a perfect example of me following my own advice: Don't wait when you see an item; if you go back, it might be gone. The price was right at $10, so even though I didn't have a current need or use for it, I tucked it into my goody closet, and one day I was inspired to take it out for a spin. I started dreaming of using it as a breakfast tray in the morning, or in the kitchen or dining room, where it was sure to make all my glasses and table linens prettier. But first, I needed to take this straightforward piece and give it a new, more stylish lease on life.

The techniques used here will result in that amazing patina of age we wish more mirrors would have. Because this technique requires using real mirror (and there are plenty of mirrors sold out there that are not!), you'll want to plan ahead for this project to have a mirror cut to size for the bottom of your tray at your local hardware or mirror store. This project works best in warm temperatures, since they will help activate the stripping solution. The magic of the *églomisé* technique is that the treatments done to the back of the mirror will show through the front.

MATERIALS

1 real mirror, cut to your desired size (see page 144)

1 bottle of mirror stripping solution

1 bottle of mirror antiquing solution

1 can of white spray lacquer

1 can of chocolate-brown spray lacquer

Two 3-inch (7.5-cm) flat foam brushes

Kraft paper

Pen or marker

400 grit sandpaper

Adhesive stencil, cut to the size of the bottom of your tray

Plastic spatula or putty knife

Medium spray bottle with a fine mist setting

Small spray bottle with a fine mist setting (such as a travel-sized perfume spritzer)

Protective gloves

Protective eyewear

4 clean, lint-free soft rags

Gentle, non-oily degreaser

Large washable plastic container

GETTING STARTED

PREPPING THE SURFACE

Once you have your pre-cut mirror (see below), remove any oils, dirt, or other buildup from it and the vintage tray.

1. Place kraft paper in the bottom of the tray, using a piece that is larger than the bottom by at least 2 inches (5 cm) on all sides.

2. Trace the shape of the bottom of the tray with a pen or marker and cut it out. Bring it to a store that sells real mirror and ask them to cut one (or two) mirrors to size for you.

3. Using a clean rag and a little degreaser, thoroughly scrub the mirror and tray.

THE REAL DEAL AT THE RIGHT SIZE *For optimal results, it's important to use real, American-made mirror (see Chapter 3, page 26). To ensure that your mirror will be a perfect fit, measure the bottom of the tray and bring the measurements to a store that sells real mirror; they will cut it to your desired size. Because real mirror is affordable, I typically ask them to make me two identical mirrors just in case I'm not completely satisfied with my first effort.*

PAINTING THE TRAY

For your safety, before you start, set up a well-ventilated, breeze-free area or spray booth (see Create Your Own Spray Booth, page 26) where you can complete all steps of this project. All of the spray lacquers and the mirror stripping and antiquing solutions require that you protect yourself from harmful fumes, so you'll also save time if you set up a command station you can return to, even if you break the project into phases over a few days.

4. Holding the spray can 10 inches (25 cm) from the surface of the tray, spray the white lacquer in long, even strokes, being careful to overlap the edges. Let the lacquer dry completely (about 45 minutes to 1 hour) before adding another coat.

5. Most surfaces need two coats of lacquer for an opaque finish. Sand the first coat when it is completely dry, and repeat steps 2 and 3 with the second coat.

STRIPPING THE MIRROR

Be sure to do these steps in a well-ventilated area while wearing protective eyewear and gloves that cover your wrists.

6 and 7. Using a flat foam brush, spread a uniform amount of stripping solution over the nonshiny back side of the mirror. Do not use too much as this can prevent the solution from activating.

8. Let the stripping solution activate for about 10 minutes. It will cause the backing paint to start bubbling up and "moving." Meanwhile, prepare the medium spray bottle with a solution of 1 part non-oily degreaser to 1 part water.

9 and 10. While the stripping solution is bubbling, cut out a sheet of kraft paper that is slightly larger than the mirror. Once all of the

1 AND 2

3

4

5

6

7

8

9

10

backing looks like it has bubbled up, place the sheet of kraft paper on top of the loosened backing paint. Lightly smooth out the kraft paper and press down so that the backing paint adheres to it.

11. Gently lift the edge of the kraft paper and remove it from the mirror. Most, if not all, of the backing paint will lift off with the kraft paper. You will likely see some leftover copper coloring—a reddish-orange color.

12. Using a clean foam brush, apply another light coat of stripping solution on the exposed silver backing of the mirror and gently agitate the solution with your brush until all of the copper color is removed and the mirror backing is a clear-white or silver color. You may need to press down a little harder with the foam brush to remove the last bits of residue.

13 and 14. Fill the plastic container half-full of water. Holding the mirror at an angle, spray on the diluted degreaser and remove the excess stripping solution on the back with a clean rag, bathing it with the water from the bath. Be very careful not to scratch the exposed silver while cleaning the back.

15. Place the wet mirror on a flat surface with the backing side facing up again. Saturate a clean rag with the mirror antiquing solution; using a patting motion, lightly sponge it over the entire exposed silver backing side. Let it activate for 15 to 20 minutes. The surface should begin to tarnish and turn a rainbow of colors as it ages and oxidizes the silver of the mirror. Check the front of the mirror to see if the tarnishing of the back side is to your taste. If not, continue to apply a little more of the mirror antiquing solution and allow it to activate until you've reached the desired appearance.

16. Using a clean rag and a clean tub of water, bathe the back of the mirror with the water to remove the antiquing solution and stop the etching process. Let the mirror dry completely (about 30 minutes) or use a fan or blow-dryer to expedite the drying process.

Mirror antiquing solution gives your mirror the look of having the silver oxidized and tarnished over time, but takes just 20 minutes. Make the tarnish less uniform so that it looks like an authentic antique.

11

12

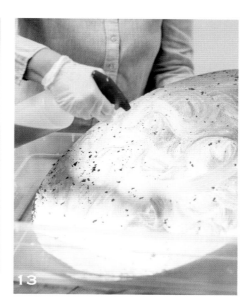

13

14

15

16

STENCILING THE TRAY

17 and 18. Remove the backing of your adhesive stencil and press it onto the back of the mirror, using a plastic spatula or putty knife to adhere it firmly.

19. Pull back the protective film on the other side of the stencil so that it leaves the negative space of your stencil pattern visible.

20. Fill a clean, large container half-full with water and set it aside. Fill the small spray bottle with antiquing solution. Set it on the fine mist setting and spray it over the stencil-covered mirror.

21. Using a clean rag, start rubbing the negative space areas of the stencil gently so that the solution cuts through the silver to the raw glass.

22. Bathe the back of the mirror in the water bath, using a clean rag to remove all of the solution. Let the mirror dry completely (about 20 to 30 minutes).

23. Remove more of the stencil so that larger sections of the design are visible on the back of the mirror.

24. In a well-ventilated area, holding the spray can 10 inches (25 cm) from the surface of the mirror, spray the chocolate-brown lacquer in long, even strokes. Let the lacquer dry completely (about 45 minutes to 1 hour).

25. With the front of the mirror facing up, replace it in the tray. The antiqued design will now be visible through the front.

Églomisé dates back at least to the Roman era. The term describes painting or etching on the back or reverse side of the glass.

17

18

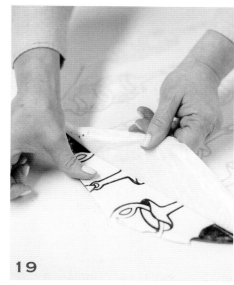

19

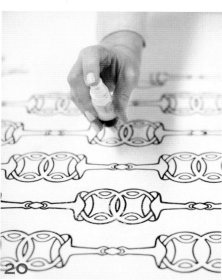

20

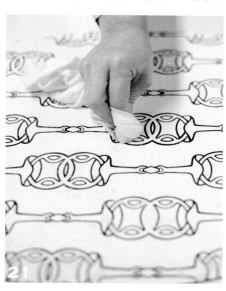

21

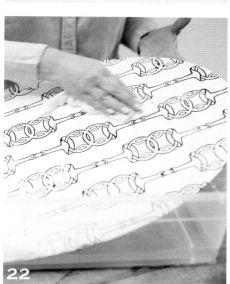

22

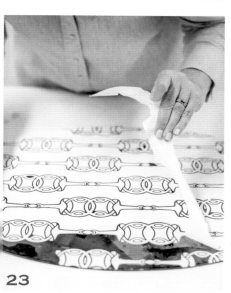

23

24

25

CHAPTER 9
AGED SURFACES

Wine gets better with age. So does furniture. It makes me inexpressibly happy that this is a common belief these days (not just among us antiques devotees!). Over the years, as we live with and love our things, they inevitably take on chips, scratches, grooves. Wood grows soft and smooth and worn. Metals take on a beautiful patina, darkened or tinged a sublime green. Paint peels and cracks, sometimes flakes off. These changes and imperfections add to the beauty of the piece in part because they reveal a sense of history. They remind us of smashingly successful dinner parties, children playing under the table, the love of a grandmother who served thousands of Sunday suppers with that precious silver before passing it along.

Whereas many of the techniques I've shown you in earlier chapters are based on adding layers—paint or waxes—on top of a piece to create the illusion of age, the projects in this chapter involve actually aging the material itself in real time. Thanks to some amazing behind-the-scenes chemistry, we can now speed up the process from decades to hours or minutes. We start with the basics—raw wood or galvanized metal, affordable as can be—and build from there. As usual, the aging can be an end in and of itself, like a classic little black dress, or it can be a means to a more fabulous end, dressed up with "accessories" like shimmering gold leaf or waxes that add a soft layer of depth or a further sense of time's gentle hand.

Reproductions are usually produced to provide a lower-cost option than the original, but finishes that look new can give them away. Convincingly aged surfaces and accents ensure a result that looks and feels more authentic.

This elegantly executed reproduction of a nineteenth-century bed was finished using milk paint and gold leaf that has been meticulously aged.

THE HARGRAVE DRESSER

Oak is such a wonderful wood for your finishing dreams and schemes! The tannins—or oils—are just right for drinking in solutions that will transform the oak with a mellow, aged finish and show off its grain. This particular dresser was found on the side of the road; it was being tossed. Maybe no one wanted the piece because it was raw wood and that seemed like too much work. By now you know that for me, it was just the opposite: an exciting canvas for the imagination. In this case, the dresser takes on a gorgeous silvery-gray style all its own.

The ultimate result shown here requires a number of steps, so it makes for a good weekend project. Don't be daunted, though; you could stop after aging the wood or adding the silver accents and your piece will still be stunning. Be sure to start with a raw wooden piece.

MATERIALS

1 container of medium-value gray wood stain or Better with Age solution

Two 8-ounce (240-ml) containers of cerusing wax

1 booklet of sterling-silver leaf, trimmed to size

1 container of light antique wax

1 container of dark antique wax

Water-based gilding size

Four 2-inch (5-cm) flat natural-bristle brushes

Slender, tapered artist's brush such as a #12 round

1 pad of #0000 steel wool (optional)

2 small squares of cardboard

3 clean, lint-free rags

GETTING STARTED

AGING THE WOOD

For this project, it's essential to start with a raw wood piece. If you want to achieve the same result on an existing piece with a stain or other finish on it, you'll need to strip it down before you begin so that you're starting with a clean slate for the solution to age. This aging technique is also meant to highlight the beauty of the grain. There is no exact substitute for the Better with Age solution, but if you can't find it, a clear, non-pigmented gray stain is an alternate finish that won't hide the wood grain as a gray paint might.

1. Dip a flat bristle brush into the Better with Age solution. Brush on the solution in long, even strokes, working from left to right and overlapping the edges of each stroke until you have covered the piece entirely. Let it dry completely (about 1 hour). The finish will be a matte gray.

ONE-STEP AGING *If you're happy with the matte gray finish from the initial staining, you can leave your piece as is—no need to seal it.*

WAXING THE WOOD

The cerusing wax adds a soft, distressed look and plays up the beautiful grain. Skip the wax on any areas where you plan to add silver leaf details.

2. Using a clean rag, apply the cerusing wax, going against the grain of the wood; this helps it seep into the grain. Squeeze more wax onto the rag as needed until you have covered the piece entirely.

3. Let the wax dry for 30 minutes. Using the steel wool, rub the wood in the direction of the grain to remove the excess wax.

4. Using a clean rag, buff the wax to your desired sheen.

CERUSING WAX *In the sixteenth century, cerusing wax—a paste that originally contained mercury—was in vogue as a beauty treatment. Nobles and royals (including Queen Elizabeth I) applied it to their faces and décolletage to achieve a pasty white look (since pale skin signified that its bearer did not have to toil away in the sun). Later, as people began to experience the toxic effects of the original substance, the passion for cerusing wax was transferred to furniture. Many of today's cerusing waxes (also known as liming waxes) are now nontoxic, and their effects on decor remain popular and desirable. If you'd like to make your own high-quality cerusing wax, mix 1 part natural calcium carbonate (chalk) in powder form (traditionally, in white, though feel free to experiment with other hues) with 2 parts all-natural squeezable beeswax until the wax has a pastelike consistency. Alternatively, you can substitute 1 part natural milk-paint powder for the chalk.*

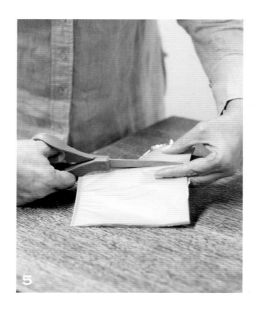

GILDING THE ACCENTS WITH SILVER LEAF

The touches of silver elevate the piece's subtlety and sophistication. If you've already waxed the whole piece, you'll need to remove the wax with a solvent like a degreaser only in the areas where you'll use the leaf. Trimming the silver leaf booklet allows you to save the rest for refinishing another piece. The finishing touches—the light and dark wax—seal the accents as well as adding to the impression of age.

5. Holding the spine of the silver leaf booklet in one hand, trim the entire booklet down to a little larger than the width of the area you're accenting, leaving room for overlap on each side.

6. Dip the artist's brush into the gilding size and remove any excess. Apply a full-coverage layer of size to the front edge of the top, in between the drawers, and at the base of the dresser. After about 15 minutes, the size solution will turn from milky-white to clear. Test the size to see if it has come to tack by touching it with the tip of your ring finger; you're looking for a gentle pull.

7. Once this tack is evident, apply a trimmed-to-size sheet of silver leaf: Holding the silver leaf booklet taut at the folded portion of tissue paper near the spine on one side and on the back of the booklet on the other side as shown, place the silver leaf against the surface and slowly pull away the single folded tissue sheet near the spine.

8. Burnish the tissue paper side of the booklet by pressing with your fingertips in one direction to adhere the silver leaf sheet below to the size, and pull the booklet away. Repeat steps 7 and 8, overlapping the edges of the leaf with the previous one, until your desired area is covered.

9. Let the size dry completely (about 1 hour after you applied it). Gently swipe away any loose shards of silver leaf with a clean flat brush. If desired, buff the silver leaf accents gently with the steel wool to expose some of the finish underneath and make the piece look more aged.

AGING THE SILVER ACCENTS

Using light and dark wax over the silver brings a hint of authenticity. As with any metallic leaf, silver leaf tends to wear away over time, and the wax imitates this effect, as well as acting as a sealant so that your silver accents will last longer. In these steps you will be waxing only the silver accents, since you previously waxed the rest of the dresser.

10 and 11. Dip a clean flat brush into the light antique wax. Remove any excess on a clean square of cardboard. Brush the wax over the silver accents. Let it dry for 10 to 15 minutes or until it comes to tack.

SEPARATE WAXING *Letting the light wax come to tack before applying the dark wax ensures that they won't blend into or muddy each other.*

12. After your light antique wax has come to tack, dip a clean flat brush into the dark antique wax and remove any excess on a clean square of cardboard.

13. Brush the dark wax over roughly 25 percent of the top of the light wax so that it adds depth without overshadowing the light, silvery highlights underneath. Let the dark wax dry for 30 minutes or until it comes to tack. Using a clean rag, buff the newly waxed areas to your desired sheen.

REWAX AND RENEW *Avoid using dusting sprays on wood. Simply rewax your piece in a year or so and you'll be able to enjoy it for years to come.*

WAX BRUSH CARE *When using waxes, it's important to clean your brushes quickly so that waxes don't set into the bristles. Use a solvent like mineral spirits, not soap and water. Let the brushes dry with the bristles up in the air. It's important not to mix up your light wax brushes and dark wax brushes; label the handles with a permanent marker. You might want to have more than one of each available so that you can put one brush in solvent when the wax starts to harden on the brush (every 5 to 10 minutes) while you continue to work with a fresh brush.*

The essential combination of light and dark waxes brushed on the silver leaf warms the accents and gives the entire piece, which is cool gray, greater warmth and depth.

THE ANDRÉ PLANTERS

France makes my heart sing. I always want to bring something home from visits there—a piece of furniture, or more often an object or an idea I can make my own. The romance of France is easy to capture with antiqued buckets filled with flowers, boxwood, or other pretty growing things. You can get the metal buckets for this project at most big-box stores. Be careful to select only the galvanized kind, not the silver-painted sort, so that your antiquing solution can work its magic directly on the zinc coating. This aging effect also works beautifully on washtubs or decorative metal letters to hang on the wall.

MATERIALS

1 bottle of zinc antiquing solution

1 booklet of gold leaf, trimmed to size (see Trimming Gold Leaf, page 50)

Indoor-outdoor stickers

Water-based gilding size

Round artist's brush (#12)

2-inch (5-cm) flat bristle brush

1 pad of #0000 steel wool (optional)

Plastic putty knife

Scissors

Protective gloves

2 or 3 clean, lint-free rags

Gentle degreaser

Small glass or plastic container

GETTING STARTED

PREPPING THE SURFACE

Oil is often used to make cutting galvanized sheet metal easier, so be sure to give your container a good cleaning to remove any grease that could act as a barrier to the antiquing solution.

1. Using a clean rag and a little degreaser, thoroughly scrub the inside and outside of the bucket.

ANTIQUING THE BUCKET

Be sure to wear gloves while working with the zinc antiquing solution. Don't forget to antique the inside of the bucket as well as the outside, since the inside top of the bucket (and sometimes more) will often be visible after you have planted something in it. You may also sometimes find yourself wanting to fill your bucket with loose flowers just as the French florists do.

2 and 3. In the glass or plastic container, saturate a clean rag in the zinc antiquing solution. Squeeze out the rag so there's not too much excess and then pat your entire surface with the zinc solution. It is best to hold the bucket at a 45-degree angle as you work your way around with the rag, rubbing in circles to cover the surface and to work in any drips. The shiny areas will start to disappear. Continue until the outside of the bucket looks completely matte black or dark gray.

4. Let the bucket air-dry. After about 15 minutes the piece will begin to dry to a beautiful dusty-gray finish, which is because the patination process has changed the metal. Let the bucket dry completely (about 15 more minutes), until there are no dark areas left. Repeat steps 2 and 3 on the inside of the bucket.

GO NONREACTIVE *It's important to use a glass or plastic container for your antiquing solution. No coffee or soup cans allowed, since the solution could react with any metal container!*

1

2

3

4

ORNAMENTING THE DETAILS

I like having decorative containers in threes, and in this case, I purchased a taller bucket with an embossed element and two smaller buckets with no ornamentation. The embossed ornament on the larger bucket catches the eye thanks to a touch of gilding. For the smaller buckets, I found an indoor-outdoor monogram sticker with a flourish that adds an element of interest and personalization. There is no need to seal the sticker for outdoor use.

5 and 6. Trim the sticker if needed. Remove the sticker backing and carefully roll the sticky side onto the upper half of the container in your preferred spot.

7. Using a plastic putty knife, burnish the sticker, pressing it well so that it adheres without bubbles.

8. Remove the backing.

SEAL AND BUFF *If you are using this technique on a zinc countertop or on decorative lettering, you can seal the sticker by rubbing a light antique wax over it with a clean, lint-free rag, letting it dry completely (about 30 minutes), then buffing it to a beautiful sheen.*

---

9. To gild the embossed element on the large bucket, dip the tip of an artist's brush into the gilding size. Remove any excess size by running the side of your brush across the lip of the container. Brush the size only on the raised areas (I did the numbers and the border around them). After about 15 minutes, the size solution will turn from milky-white to clear. Test the size to see if it has come to tack by touching it with the tip of your ring finger; you're looking for a gentle pull.

10 and 11. Once the size has come to tack, apply a trimmed-to-size sheet of gold leaf: Holding the gold-leaf booklet taut at the folded portion of tissue paper near the spine on one side and at the other edge as shown, place the gold leaf against the surface and slowly pull away the single folded tissue sheet near the spine. Burnish the tissue paper side of the booklet by pressing with your fingertips in one direction to adhere the gold-leaf sheet below to the size, and pull the booklet away. Repeat, overlapping the edge of each leaf, until the desired areas are covered in gold leaf.

12. Let the size dry completely (about an hour after you applied it). Gently swipe away any loose shards of gold leaf with the flat brush.

13. If you would like to dull the shine of the leaf to age it, rub gently with the steel wool. Buff with a clean rag.

Fill your buckets with loose fresh flowers as the French florists do.

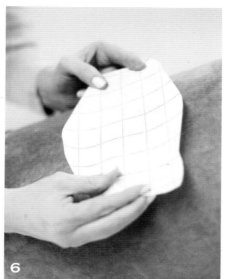

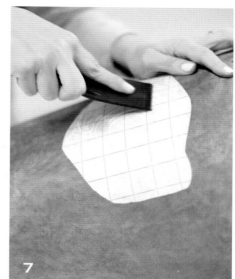

Round or square, roomy or petite, containers like this one illustrate the alluring combination of aged zinc and fresh greenery.

CHAPTER 10
TRANSFERS

My love for découpage hails back to the early seventies, when I would decorate wooden purses and plaques with all kinds of cut-outs. It was probably no surprise that years later, I would revisit one of my first loves, one that connects me to a long history of avid crafty folk. Some of the earliest known occurrences of what we call découpage appear on ancient tombs in East Siberia; the technique is then believed to have been developed in Asia before moving to Europe, where it peaked in popularity in the eighteenth century (with such reported fans as Marie Antoinette and Madame de Pompadour). Most often, traditional découpage involved applying paper cut-outs to a surface. The projects that follow offer a twist on the technique: Here we are transferring the image onto a surface and wiping the paper away, which is why I call these *transfers*. In both cases, the goal is the same: to apply an image or pattern (or words, if you like) to a surface.

The ability to cut and adhere, or to magically transfer, an image is exciting because it allows for endless customization. The only limits are your imagination and your ability to print your desired image on copy paper—which is to say, almost no limits these days! And transfers or découpage suit an incredible number of surfaces: wood, glass, resin, metal, even some fabrics. It may be true that not everyone can paint a museum-worthy work of art or take an award-winning photograph or dream up a stylish pattern. But I believe that everyone is artistic. Simply follow your eye and your heart to an image that speaks to you, transfer it, and you'll bring something old to life or create something entirely new that you'll be proud and happy to see every day in your home.

No time to become a lettering artist? Transfers provide quick and easy results and offer endless opportunities for creating different styles.

It doesn't take much for even the most ordinary objects to become extraordinary. With a little milk paint and a decorative transfer, this terra-cotta pot looks like it came straight from the antiques shop.

THE CAROLINE HEADBOARD

That spot at the head of your bed is crying out for something beautiful, but the months are slipping by without a solution. Maybe all the headboards you've considered seem too bulky or too expensive or you're just not sure which direction to take. Here's a simple remedy that allows you to tailor the look to what's already in your bedroom, or maybe even to inspire a fresh decor scheme if you haven't achieved your ideal bedroom style. Here I was going for a playful bohemian look that mixes pattern on pattern with the pillows, but because you are découpaging the planks with the image of your choice, the options are infinite—French Provençal, midcentury modern, art deco, animal print, you name it. The découpage glue needs ample time to dry, so give yourself several hours for this project, or preferably overnight.

MATERIALS

¼-inch- (6-mm-) thick raw wood boards (preferably oak) in your preferred width and height to create your desired headboard shape (the white oak boards shown are 5 inches [13 cm] wide and 2½ to 3½ feet [76 to 106 cm] in length)

1 quart (960 ml) of white chalk-based paint

1 bottle of white cerusing wax

1 bottle of transfer solution or découpage glue

Two 3-inch (7.5-cm) flat foam brushes

Image of your choice, printed on a laser printer on 100# paper and cut to size

3 or 4 clean, lint-free rags

Small washable container

GETTING STARTED

PREPPING THE SURFACE

A single coat of chalk-based paint creates a nice, clean base for your découpage images. As long as you are using clean raw wood, you do not need to do the typical degreasing step first.

1. Dip a foam brush into the chalk-based paint. Remove any excess paint by running the side of your brush across the inner lip of the can. Apply the paint to the wood in long, even strokes that overlap at the edges. Allow the paint to dry completely (about 20 to 30 minutes).

PLAY WITH COLOR *You can play around with the color of your base coat of paint, which will show through the découpage. Other great options that won't overwhelm your image include grays and soft blues or pinks. If you like the idea of going bolder, try a tartan plaid image on top of a black or forest-green painted base!*

DÉCOUPAGING THE BOARDS

Because of the length of the boards, you will probably need to print and trim several pages of images or words and lay them end to end to cover each board. Don't worry about making them perfect. I encourage you to work on découpaging only one board at a time, though, to ensure the best adhesion with the board.

2. In the washable container, dip a clean foam brush into the découpage glue and remove any excess. Apply the glue evenly to the board and to the front of the paper with the image on it, not the blank back. Before you proceed, be sure there are no "holidays" (gaps) in the glue coverage or the image won't transfer completely.

3. Adhere the front of the paper to the board, pressing out any bumps. Repeat with the rest of your images and boards. Let them dry completely (at least 2½ to 3 hours or preferably overnight).

4. Once the découpage glue is completely dry, saturate a clean rag with warm tap water, squeezing out any excess. In a counterclockwise circular motion, rub the wet rag over the entire wood segment. You may need to wet the rag more than once. As pellets of paper start coming off the surface, gently remove them and the pattern or image will emerge clearly. Repeat with the rest of the images and boards. Let them dry completely (at least an hour).

WAXING THE BOARDS

A soft white cerusing wax helps give the découpaged image subtle depth without too much shine. You could do a light and dark wax combination if you prefer a more aged finish.

5. Squeeze some cerusing wax directly onto a découpaged board. Using a clean rag, rub the wax evenly over the entire surface in a circular motion. Repeat with the rest of the boards.

6. Let the wax dry completely (about 1 hour). Using a clean rag, buff it to a soft shine. Attach the boards to a frame or apply them directly onto the wall.

DELIA PALLET ART

By now you know that a big part of the Rescue Restore Redecorate lifestyle is recognizing the beauty in what others might throw away. This project takes that idea literally, repurposing the kind of pallets for wine or groceries that many stores would put out on the curb. Many of these pallets are made of oak, one of my favorite woods to antique because of its lovely grain and its reactivity with aging solutions and waxes.

Here we treat pieces of the pallet as our materials for an artistic composition. No doubt you've come across lots of amazing frames as you hunt through markets; if you've ever wondered what to put in one, here's an option that can be customized to your heart's content. You can treat the pallet wood inside with different finishes you've learned in previous projects and swap in any image or pattern that you love for the plaid and flowers I used. A whole pallet wall done in this technique would be adorable for a nursery, would brighten up a laundry room, or would provide a wonderful surprise between shelves in a bookcase (naturally, one that you've rescued!). Plan ahead with this project; it's best to give the découpage glue several hours or—if possible—a full night's sleep to dry.

MATERIALS

1/4- or 1/8-inch- (6-mm- or 3-mm-) thick raw hardwood segments (preferably white or red oak)

1 bottle of clear, non-pigmented gray wood stain, such as Better with Age solution

1 quart (960 ml) of white chalk-based paint

1 bottle of transfer solution or découpage glue

1 bottle of zinc antiquing solution

Venetian plaster powder (about 1 cup [240 ml])

Images of your choice, printed on a laser printer on copy or 100# paper and cut to size

Galvanized metal letters or design of your choice

Two 2-inch (5-cm) flat bristle brushes

Two 3-inch (7.5-cm) flat foam brushes

Metal trowel

2 or 3 clean, lint-free rags

Small glass or plastic container

Plastic fork or blender (see For Paint Only, page 18)

Hot-glue gun and glue stick

GETTING STARTED

AGING THE WOOD

I aged some of my wood pieces with the Better with Age solution (as an alternative you can use a medium-value gray wood stain) and stopped there; others I then treated with the Venetian plaster for contrast. There's no need to age the pieces you'll be découpaging with images. Using varied lengths of wood adds interest to the overall piece. I usually age all of the pieces at once, though you could do them in batches so that the aging solution doesn't dry too much before you add the plaster.

The Better with Age solution highlights the wood grain in a soft gray color. If you can't find Better with Age, a cerusing wax is an alternative finish that allows the wood grain to show through. These waxes typically offer a cloudy-white finish; to make your own gray cerusing wax, see the sidebar on page 154.

I. Dip a bristle brush into the Better with Age solution. Remove any excess by running the side of your brush across the inner lip of the container. Apply the solution to the wood in long, even strokes, working from left to right. Let it dry about 75 percent (for 10 to 15 minutes). The wood will begin to turn a dark gray.

2. Using a plastic fork or in a blender, mix I part Venetian plaster powder with I part warm tap water until it has reached a sour cream consistency. When the wood is still moist but has dried about 75 percent, apply the plaster mixture to the wood with a clean bristle brush. Let it dry partially for 3 to 4 minutes.

PLASTER TIPS *Applying the plaster while the wood is still moist allows the aging solution to age the plaster as well. You can also colorize your plaster by mixing in natural milk paint or other natural paint pigment.*

3. Using the metal trowel at a 45-degree angle, press firmly, dragging the trowel across the wood from right to left to expose the wood grain.

CREATING THE IMAGE/PATTERN PANELS

To add further contrast and intrigue to the beautiful woods, search the web to find images you love. The images shown were printed on regular copy paper, but you can use a 100# paper to make the découpaging process a little easier.

4. Print and trim the images of your choice to the size of your wood segments.

5. Dip a foam brush into the chalk paint, removing any excess. Apply an even layer of paint to the boards you will be using with the transfer images. Let it dry completely (about 20 to 30 minutes).

6. Dip a clean foam brush into the découpage glue, removing any excess. Apply the glue evenly to the board and to the front of the paper with the image on it, not the blank back. Before you proceed, be sure there are no "holidays" (gaps) in the glue coverage or the image won't transfer completely. Adhere the front of the paper to the board, pressing out any bumps. Repeat with the rest of your images and boards. Let them dry completely (at least 2½ to 3 hours or preferably overnight).

7. Once the découpage glue is completely dry, saturate a clean rag with warm tap water, squeezing out any excess, and rub the wet rag over the entire wood segment. You may need to wet the rag more than once. As pellets of paper start coming off the surface, gently remove them and the pattern or image will emerge clearly. Repeat with the rest of the images and boards. Let them dry completely (at least an hour).

8. Laying out your finished pieces can be like assembling a puzzle. Allow the textures and colors to complement each other.

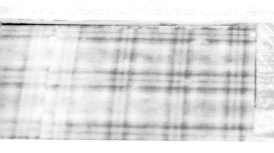

ANTIQUING THE LETTERS

I got the galvanized sheet-metal word "family" from Etsy, then aged it to have a similar feeling to the rest of my pallet art. After the metal letters were dry, I attached them to the finished pallet art using hot glue.

9 and 10. In a glass or plastic container, saturate a clean rag in the zinc antiquing solution. Squeeze out any excess, and then pat all surfaces of the letters with the solution. The shiny areas will start to disappear. Continue until the letters look completely matte black or dark gray. Let them dry completely (about 30 minutes) until the finish is dusty-gray and there are no dark areas left. Attach with hot glue.

FRAME IT *You can assemble your art on a piece of luan wood (⅛ inch [3 mm] thick) cut to size for your frame.*

"Family" means many things to many people. How much fun would it be to do a project with your family?

CHAPTER 11
CRAFTING A BEAUTIFUL LIFE

Our homes are an extension of ourselves, so it's no wonder that we want to live surrounded by things we love, and that when we have guests, we want them to see who we are and what we cherish. On our journey together, we've built a repertoire of finishes that you can use to age and embellish, personalize and customize your very own treasures. I'm sure that they will become conversation pieces—and I want you to enjoy the bragging rights! But I also know it's never just about one glorious piece of furniture or one object. After we rescue and restore, we redecorate with what we've created—and that's where the ensemble comes in. Even though we want our pieces to stand out, we tend to feel most comfortable in rooms that seem collected and balanced, no matter which period the pieces come from. There's so much to say about how to create such a room; here are a few of my favorite principles as you begin the next stage of your *Rescue, Restore, Redecorate* journey.

How many techniques can you find in this picture from the projects in this book that you have read about and made? (Find out on page 184.) When the items and finishes are strategically brought together, you are "crafting a beautiful life."

A CLASSIC HOME FEELS COLLECTED

Instead of worrying that your furniture must match or represent the same historical period or style, aim for a well-balanced ensemble of textures, shapes, tones, and colors. If you start with a majority of clean, neutral elements—the major furniture in the room such as the sofa or the floors or the curtains—and then add color through the accessories, you will find that the ensemble looks intentional (as well as being flexible when you want to swap in a new accent color on pillows and tabletop objects, for example). Once you've put this kind of neutral backdrop in place, you can have fun introducing variety through your furniture and details. Look at pieces that share similar lines even if their finishes, their eras, or their origins differ. Call it my art education, but I love French and English furniture—pieces that are classic and timeless. The clean lines of a midcentury modern cabinet in a bold color can beautifully complement an ornate lamp, just as a matte chalk-painted chair can balance the shine of a lacquered table.

THE STYLE PILE *The following exercise is helpful when you are still training your eye and sussing out your design style:*

Focusing on rooms that intrigue you or that stick in your mind, tear at least twenty pages out of interiors magazines. Lay them out on the floor and glance through them until patterns start to emerge (I promise, they will). Are you attracted to calm settings with occasional bright pops of color? Deep, earthy tones and a mix of textures? Straight lines and transparent surfaces? Comfy furniture and layers of want-to-fall-right-into-it softness? Your preferences will help guide you in making smart but heart-driven purchases as well as revealing what kind of finishes interest you most.

Every house needs an eclectic room.

This dining room not only mixes styles; notice the furnishings, too: The formal Italian mirror is an antique. I love the texture that the French credenza, which has been stripped and bleached, adds to the room. The chairs are a mix of styles, periods, and woods, including painted Venetian chairs from the eighteenth century. Fine antiques and rescued pieces in a multitude of finishes blend in an eclectic room that is both impressive and easy to enjoy.

Number of finishes: four—milk paint, antique mirrors, gilding, and staining

LITTLE TOUCHES HAVE A BIG IMPACT

We spend so much time picking out the perfect sofa or dining table; rightfully so. Too often, however, we forget how important the accessories are in making a room look and feel complete. Unassuming little objects and artworks placed here and there are often the glue for the whole design. If you examine any corner of a well-designed room, you will see how accessories work with the furniture to set the scene. If you view the entire room through this lens, you'll soon realize that what you thought was unattainable beauty can be broken down into several smaller and easier-to-accomplish designs that create the well-balanced symphony of color, texture, and line that you so admire.

ANTIQUES INFUSE MAGIC

Maybe this goes without saying by now, but the antiques you've restored (and the "antiques" you've created with aging and faux finishes) will transform your rooms. Even if you don't know the history of a piece, you have a new, riveting story to tell about how you've rescued and refinished it—and brought it to new life. I've encouraged you throughout the book to see the potential in rescues; now I encourage you to see the potential in what you've restored. While I often decide how I will finish a piece based on where it will go and what would look nice in that environment, I am always open to changes during the restoring process. I might change my mind and use a different color paint or a different kind of wax along the way. Sometimes, after I see the finished piece, it's clear it "wants" to go somewhere I hadn't imagined! Try the restored item in a different spot or even a different room. You may have lowered the financial stakes with your curbside and flea market shopping, but I encourage you never to underestimate the value you've added to your pieces with love and your own two hands.

SEE YOUR HOME AS A WORK IN PROGRESS

You may not have a choice but to follow this principle if you're like me and are constantly falling for a new vase or chair or other goodies you see in your shopping excursions! Upgrading is wonderful . . . and so is editing. A room can have too much "jewelry" (in the form of accessories or ornate furniture or textures) just as a person can. Instead, feature one or two stand-out pieces of furniture or objects in a room. Give them the space to tell their story—and yours.

***

My hope is that the ideas in this book have sparked your passion for rescuing, restoring, and redecorating. I invite you to continue the journey, to create more pieces and more stories; I can't wait to see and hear them, but more important, I can't wait for you to discover them for yourself.

Antiques that you rescue in your treasure hunts—like these eighteenth-century torchères—add beauty and intrigue to your home, and tell a visual story of a life well lived.

THE REFINISHER'S VERNACULAR

ANTIQUING: the process of searching for antiques, or—as often used in refinishing circles and this book—creating a sense of age on a piece through the use of refinishing techniques

BURNISH: to cause to adhere (e.g., gold leaf during the gilding process) and/or make smooth and shiny through rubbing

CALCIUM CARBONATE: one of the main components of chalk, and an alternate name for chalk-based paints

CASEIN: the main protein in milk, and an alternate name for milk-based paints

CERUSING: a type of wax that offers a soft, cloudy finish; also called liming wax (see Cerusing Wax, page 154)

DOUBLE PROCESSING: brushing over paint that has already begun to dry, often causing an undesirable bumpy or uneven finish; to be avoided

ÉGLOMISÉ: a technique based on etching, painting, or otherwise treating the reverse side of a piece of glass, such as a mirror; also called reverse painting

FLY SPEC: watermarking

GILDING: the technique of covering a material with a thin layer of gold; may also be used to refer to a similar application of silver or other metal alloys meant to look like precious metals

HOLIDAY: a gap in coverage, such as on a painted or gilded surface; to be avoided

OFFLOAD: to remove the excess, such as with paint or wax on a brush

OXIDATION OR PATINATION: a chemical process that typically occurs when a metal, stone, wood, or other material reacts to the air, often over a long period of time; often resulting in a change in color and considered desirable by many for the impression of age it conveys, it can also be achieved in a short period of time with certain chemical solutions (see Chapter 9: Aged Surfaces, page 151)

SIZE: a glue used in the gilding process (see also *tack*)

SURFACTANT: an agent on a surface that reduces the ability to add paint, gilding, or other finishes; surfactants, such as cleaning residue, oil, or grease, are common on vintage or previously used mass-produced pieces and are to be removed to ensure a clean slate for optimal restoring and refinishing results

TACK: in gilding, a desirable state for the application of gold (or other metallic) leaf, identifiable when the originally milky-white gilding size has turned clear and slightly sticky; in waxing, a desirable state for buffing, identifiable when the wax has partially dried and become slightly sticky

ACKNOWLEDGMENTS

I am so blessed to have worked with the best of the best on this book. My dream photographer had always been Quentin Bacon. I had the chills the first day we met.

To Jill Cohen, literally the hardest-working woman I know. She amazes me and is truly an inspiration to me daily. I am so grateful to also call her my friend.

To Doug Turshen, my amazing designer. His eye and aesthetic makes me feel like we are kindred spirits. I still think about the first time we met; I teared up and got chill bumps. To my writers Tarra and Aliza, for taking my thoughts and musings and giving them a cohesive voice.

To my team for making this book all possible. Alex, Krystal, Kelsey, Annabella, Chandler, Christian, and Terri. I love being your mother maker.

To Debbi Fields Rose, for being my mentor and true-blue friend.

I want to thank my children, Brooke, Megan, Stephanie, and Preston, for being understanding during all the long hours and for helping me during your summer vacations (even though you were sure there were child labor laws!). Your passions encourage me more than you will ever know.

To my parents, for loving me and teaching me to work hard and never give up on my dreams. For loving each other for seventy-three years and giving me an example of commitment and a couple that works together.

I am so grateful that the Lord has brought into my life the opportunity to help rescue and restore furniture, homes, and more, and to see the beauty in things that have been tossed away.

Editor: Shawna Mullen
Designer: Doug Turshen with David Huang
Production Manager: Rebecca Westall

Library of Congress Control Number: 2017944960

ISBN: 978-1-4197-2901-0
eISBN: 978-1-68335-228-0

Printed and bound in China
10 9 8 7 6 5 4 3 2 1

Abrams books are available at special discounts when purchased in
quantity for premiums and promotions as well as fundraising or
educational use. Special editions can also be created to specification. For
details, contact specialsales@abramsbooks.com or the address below.

ABRAMS The Art of Books
195 Broadway, New York, NY 10007
abramsbooks.com